The
Justin Wilson
Gourmet and Gourmand
Cookbook

The Justin Wilson Gourmet and Gourmand Cookbook

Let me tole you how come the reason for the title "Gourmet and Gourmand Cookbook." A gourmet is an epicure, a person who loves to eat well-prepared food. A gourmand is just a P-I-G hog. Me, I'm both.

Pelican Publishing Company

GRETNA 1985

First printing, June 1984
Second printing, December 1984
Third printing, April 1985

Library of Congress Cataloging in Publication Data

Wilson, Justin.
  The Justin Wilson gourmet and gourmand cookbook.

  Includes index.
  1. Cookery, American—Louisiana.   2. Louisiana—
Social life and customs.   I. Title.
TX715.W74934   1984   641.59763   83-13376
ISBN 0-88289-430-7

Photographs by Jeannine Meeds Wilson, except cover and page 6 by Ed and Shirley Craig.

Manufactured in the United States of America

Published by Pelican Publishing Company, Inc.
1101 Monroe Street, Gretna, Louisiana 70053

CONTENTS

You can tell by the way my wife Jeannine and I look that the people ate all the food—and it was good!

FOREWORD

He looks like a Southern colonel or someone you might have met on a river-boat who wanted to teach you this new game, "poker." The face is handsome, the eyebrows dance when he talks.

It is when he talks that you know you've never met anyone quite like him. He's an original, a one of a kind, and thousands upon thousands of people have laughed as they never laughed before when he tells his stories—tales about the most unique people who inhabit our earth, the great Cajuns of South Louisiana.

As he simultaneously murders both the French and the English language, a people come alive. You can see them before your eyes, on the bayous, standing over a barbecue pit, having a cold one, getting ready for the Mardi Gras.

He brings to life their wit, their charm, and their unbelievable capacity to make of life, come what may, the best!

He does it with a leer, a smile, a booming laugh, a question, a phrase, a word followed by an exclamation point or a question mark.

He is the best, and to know him is to love not only him, but the people he has helped to make legend.

Justin Wilson is, above all else, an artist.

He is also an artist when it comes to cooking. He can work the same magic with fish and fowl, with vegetables and fruit, as he can with language.

He loves to cook. His mission in life seems to be to make people enjoy life, to make them laugh, and to make them eat.

This book is a collection of some of his new recipes. It is probably the most unusual cookbook you will ever own. As you read, as you add a dash of salt and a little pepper, you will understand Justin Wilson, and you will be grateful that you have come to know him.

GUS WEILL

This book is dedicated to my wife, Jeannine.
Without her it would not have been written.

The
Justin Wilson
Gourmet and Gourmand
Cookbook

HOW TO MAKE A ROUX

Plain flour

Oil—bacon drippings, olive oil, cooking oil, lard, or a combination of these.

I use 2 or 3 parts of flour to 1 part oil. If I want a t'ick, t'ick roux, I use 3 parts flour to 1 part oil. If I want a t'in roux, I use 2 parts flour to 1 part oil.

Mix flour and oil in a heavy pot. A black iron skillet or a Magnalite skillet works best. Cook slowly as the roux changes from a cream color all the way to the color of a Hershey chocolate bar. You got to stir the roux damn near all the time while it cook itself. Me, I got a special roux stirring spoon for dat, and I don't use it for something none at all except for stirring my roux. The way I make a roux it takes from 45 minutes to more than one hour before it's did. And how come the reason for that is because I want to cook the flour taste out of it.

Now some peoples say, "I cook my roux in a microwave oven." I want to tole you that I have, too, cooked a roux in a microwave oven. And it don't make some difference to me. You can cook a roux a lot of different ways. But this way that I'm just tole you has worked for me more than 50 years, and it work for many other peoples around South Louisiana. Also, too, it taste more better.

After my roux is cooked all the way plum', it got a shine on it (sorta like the shine the sunset make on Colyell Bay when the water ain't too muddy). I add my chopped vegetables like onion, bell pepper, and celery. With bell pepper and celery, you got to be careful. They are taste killers, so don't use too much. Don't worry about using too much onion. After the vegetables have cooked awhile and the onions are clear, put in chopped parsley and green onions. I put in a little cold water and then add fresh garlic (chopped up). I'm stirring all the time.

Now add all the other things what you need to make you gumbo, you sauce piquant, or you brown gravy hash or stew.

Appetizers

Andouille à la Jeannine
Oyster Paté
Calf Liver Paté
Hot Crab Dip à la Gloria
Crawfish or Shrimp Cocktail
Leftover Meat Spread or Salad
Mushrooms Sautéed in Bacon Drippings

This crab dip à la Gloria was named for a lady in North Carolina, and we did a little Cajun messing with this and it taste real good.

ANDOUILLE À LA JEANNINE

1 cup dry white wine
2 lbs. andouille or smoked sausage

2 TBS. honey
1 TBS. creole mustard

Slice andouille 1/4-to 1/2-inch thick. Mix all liquid ingredients and pour over andouille in a covered skillet. Cook over low heat until andouille is tender.

Andouille is gumbo sausage for all you peoples who live away from the center of the universe. You can use other sausage and it would taste okay.

OYSTER PATÉ

1 quart oysters (retain liquid)
1/4 tsp. garlic powder
1 tsp. Louisiana hot sauce
1/2 tsp. onion powder

1 TBS. Lea & Perrins Worcestershire sauce
Water (just enough to cover oysters)
Salt, to taste

Cook oysters in their own juice with all above ingredients. In food processor, put olives (stuffed with pimentos), oysters (drained), bacon (and a little bacon drippings), shake of garlic and onion powders, shake of chili powder, and sweet relish. Pulverize well in food processor. Chill and serve on crackers.

CALF LIVER PATÉ

Liver, already cooked
Bread and butter pickles or sweet
   pickles
Olives stuffed with pimentos

Salt
Louisiana hot sauce
Salad dressing (optional)
Bacon and bacon drippings

Grind all ingredients except salt, Louisiana hot sauce and salad dressing in food processor. Add the latter ingredients and mix well.

T'ank goodness for dat food processor. It know its business, I garontee!

HOT CRAB DIP À LA GLORIA

Equal parts of crabmeat and
   Philadelphia cream cheese
Louisiana hot sauce

Lime Juice
Chopped pecans
Salt

Go through the crabmeat with your hands in a colander to get the shells out. After cheese is at room temperature, combine all ingredients in a bowl. Add salt and Louisiana hot sauce to taste. Serve hot in a chafing dish. Use amount of pecans that you like—but not too many, though.

We say, use you' hands because dat's de firs' fork you had, an' besides you can feel wit' dem.

CRAWFISH OR SHRIMP COCKTAIL

Sauce:
1/2 cup Heinz chili sauce
1/2 cup catsup
1/2 cup horseradish
1 TBS. Lea & Perrins Worcestershire
   sauce

1/2 tsp. salt
1 TBS. lemon or lime juice
1/2 cup parsley, chopped fine
Louisiana hot sauce, to taste
Boiled crawfish or shrimp

Combine all ingredients to make sauce. Pour over crawfish or shrimp, or dip the crawfish or shrimp in the sauce.

LEFTOVER MEAT SPREAD OR SALAD

Leftover meat (any one or a mixture of beef, pork, chicken, venison, lamb, etc.)
Hard-boiled eggs, as many as you like
Dill pickles, to taste
All these ingredients in any proportion you like, grind and chop fine in the food processor

Mayonnaise, to taste
Durkee's dressing, if you like, to taste
India relish, to taste
Louisiana hot sauce, to taste
Lea & Perrins Worcestershire, to taste
Salt, again, to taste

Mix all of this in a mixing bowl and make sandwiches or serve as a salad. Leave mayonnaise and Durkee's out and this can be frozen in portions and used with mayonnaise when wanted.

MUSHROOMS SAUTÉED IN BACON DRIPPINGS

2 lbs. fresh mushrooms
1/2 cup bacon drippings
1 cup dry white wine
2 TBS. soy sauce

1/4 tsp. cayenne pepper
1 TBS. lemon or lime juice
1 tsp. salt
1/2 tsp. garlic powder

Put all ingredients including mushrooms in a big skillet or frying pan. Sauté on medium heat until mushrooms are tender.

We use dem bacon drippings in this recipe because there are usually drippings that peoples don't know w'at to did wit', an' it a shame to waste dem.

Making potato salad without potatoes. It tastes more better when it gets on your elbow.

Salads and Sauces

Leftover Fish Salad
Leftover French Fried Potato Salad
Potato Salad without Potatoes à la Mrs. Vol Dooley
Boiled Asparagus for Salad
Broccoli and Artichoke Heart Salad
Elbow Macaroni Salad
Egg Salad
Minced Ham and Egg Salad
Bacon Potato Salad
Egg Salad and Crushed Crackers
4, or 5, or 6, or More Bean Salad
Justin's Salad Dressing
Sauce à la Jeannine
Remoulade Sauce

LEFTOVER FISH SALAD

Boned fish—whatever you have left
  over
Chopped hard-boiled eggs — as many
  as you like
Mayonnaise, to taste

Poupon mustard, to taste
Louisiana hot sauce
2 TBS. onions, chopped
2 TBS. dill relish
Salt, to taste

Mix all ingredients and serve as a salad or sandwich spread.

LEFTOVER FRENCH FRIED POTATO SALAD

French fries, cubed
Salad dressing (not mayonnaise)
Black olives, chopped
Green olives with pimentos, chopped
Celery, chopped
Sweet relish

Dill relish
Louisiana hot sauce
Onions, chopped
Or . . . any other things you like in salad
Amounts depend on leftover french
  fries

Jus' find a big enough bowl, then mix everything together until it starts to mingle itself real well.

POTATO SALAD WITHOUT POTATOES
À LA MRS. VOL DOOLEY

4 stay-fresh bags saltine crackers
1 cup celery, chopped
1 cup onions, chopped
1 cup sweet relish or sweet pickles,
   chopped
1 cup dill relish or dill pickles, chopped
Salad dressing (not mayonnaise)

6 hard-boiled eggs, chopped
Louisiana hot sauce, to taste
1 cup and more pimento olives,
   chopped
1 cup black olives, chopped
1 cup green onions (optional)

Crumble crackers and mix all ingredients in a large bowl. Add salad dressing to the desired consistency. If you serve the next day, you might have to add more salad dressing because the crackers drink up all those tasty juices.

BOILED ASPARAGUS FOR SALAD

1-1/2 lbs. fresh green asparagus
1-1/2 TBS. fresh lime juice
1 TBS. wine vinegar
1 TBS. soy sauce
1 tsp. Louisiana hot sauce

3 TBS. good olive oil
Water, of course
Salt, to taste—but watch it, soy sauce
   is salty

Wash asparagus spears thoroughly (don't scrub). Trim off tough part but save and cook along with top part of spears as it helps to flavor. Then boil until tender, but don't boil too fast.

You don't got to put dese in salad, you can jus' eat dem.

I want to tole you that Carl Fry, the director-producer of my television cooking show, took over my place on the show and finished the meal for me.

BROCCOLI AND ARTICHOKE HEART SALAD

1/2 cup olive oil
1 lime (juice of)
1 lemon (juice of)
2 tsp. Louisiana hot sauce
1 large or 2 small cloves of garlic
Lea & Perrins Worcestershire sauce
5 drops Peychaud's bitters

Salt to cover garlic
2 TBS. wine vinegar
3 to 4 lbs. fresh broccoli, cut in pieces
2 cans (8-1/2 oz.) artichoke hearts,
　quartered
Tomatoes (fresh)—1 or 2 large, cubed
2 TBS. green onions or chives, chopped

Mash garlic with salt, using a table fork. This works well in a large wooden bowl. Add olive oil, stir; add hot sauce, stir; add Lea & Perrins, stir; add bitters, stir; add lime and lemon, stir; add vinegar, stir. Parboil broccoli just enough to keep from being tough. Put broccoli, artichoke hearts, chives, and tomatoes into dressing and mix well. Let set for at least 1 hour.

ELBOW MACARONI SALAD

1 lb. elbow macaroni
1 cup onions, chopped fine
1 cup dill pickles, chopped fine
1/2 cup green onions, chopped fine
1 cup sweet pickles, chopped fine
1-1/2 cups celery, chopped fine
1 cup fresh parsley (stems and leaves),
　chopped fine
1 cup olives, including pimentos,
　chopped fine

1 cup bell pepper, chopped fine
1 cup cheddar cheese, grated
2 cups hard-boiled eggs, chopped fine
1 cup salad dressing or mayonnaise
4 TBS. yellow mustard
Cayenne pepper or Louisiana hot
　sauce, to taste
Salt, to taste
2 TBS. olive oil
2 TBS. lemon juice

Cook macaroni until done. Cool. Combine in a bowl with all dry ingredients. Mix salad dressing or mayonnaise with mustard, Louisiana hot sauce, olive oil, and lemon juice. Blend this in the dry ingredients. If it is still too dry, add additional mayonnaise or salad dressing. Refrigerate for 1 day before serving.

EGG SALAD

—————————◆—————————

Hard-boiled eggs

Dill pickle relish

Zatarain creole mustard or poupon

Salad dressing or mayonnaise

Sweet pickle relish

Louisiana hot sauce

Salt to taste

Mash eggs fine with a fork or food processor. Add sweet relish and dill relish, or use your food processor to chop pickles up fine. Add mustard and stir. Then add mayonnaise, Louisiana hot sauce and salt to taste. Stir to mix well.

MINCED HAM AND EGG SALAD

—————————◆—————————

6 hard-boiled eggs

2 lbs. ham, chopped

Mayonnaise, to taste

Salt

Louisiana hot sauce, to taste

Dill pickles, to taste, chopped

Pimento, chopped

Chop eggs and ham in food processor and salt to taste. Add mayonnaise, hot sauce, and chopped dill pickles and chopped pimento to taste.

Let me tole you r'at now, this food processor is a smart alexander for true.

BACON POTATO SALAD

8 cups potatoes, boiled and cooled
1/2 lb. bacon drippings and crisp fried
    bacon, crumbled
1 cup onions, chopped
1 cup celery, chopped
1 cup dill pickles, chopped

1 cup sweet pickles, chopped
1/2 cup yellow mustard
Salt to taste
Mayonnaise, to taste
2 tsp. Louisiana hot sauce

Peel and mash potatoes. Add bacon drippings and everything else.

If you don't know w'at bacon drippings are, you better not mess with this recipe.

EGG SALAD AND CRUSHED CRACKERS

Sweet pickles, chopped, to taste
Dill pickles, chopped, to taste
Mustard or Durkee's dressing, to taste
Mayonnaise, to taste
Louisiana hot sauce, to taste
Salt, to taste

Lea & Perrins Worcestershire sauce,
    to taste
6 eggs mashed up or chopped in food
    processor
Crackers

Make egg salad. Crush crackers and mix together. The reason for the crackers is twicefold—it stretches the amount (like adding water to soup or gumbo) and it changes the flavor somewhat.

Use dat food processor.

This is my favorite wooden bowl for mixing a salad. I been having the vegetables marinate for a long time.

4, OR 5, OR 6, OR MORE BEAN SALAD

1 #2 can black-eyed peas, drained
1 #2 can red beans, drained
1 #2 can green beans, drained
1 #2 can wax beans, drained

1 #2 can lima beans, drained
1 #2 can garbanzo beans, drained
1 cup onions, sliced

Use Justin's salad dressing—mix dressing early.
Combine all beans and put in onion slices, then pour Justin's salad dressing over top.

You can make this the day before and refrigerate so that the flavors mingle themselves real good.

JUSTIN'S SALAD DRESSING

1 large clove garlic
Salt to crush garlic
4 TBS. olive oil
1 tsp. Louisiana hot sauce
2 tsp. Lea & Perrins Worcestershire
  sauce

1 TBS. lime or lemon juice, fresh
2 tsp. wine vinegar
2 TBS. creole mustard or poupon

Using a fork in a wooden bowl, crush garlic with salt. Pour in olive oil and mix well. Combine other ingredients in order listed, mixing well after each one.

Prepare to use with green tossed salad or bean salad.

SAUCE À LA JEANNINE

1 TBS. olive oil
1 8-oz. package cream cheese at room
   temperature
1 tsp. Lea & Perrins Worcestershire
   sauce

1 tsp. Louisiana hot sauce
Pimento olives (salad olives) and a
   little juice
Crisp bacon, crumbled
Dry white wine

Heat olive oil slightly in bottom of double boiler. Add cream cheese to oil and melt and beat together. After oil and cheese are well combined, add Worcestershire and Louisiana hot sauce and olives in some juice of themselves. Then if it needs a little more liquid, put in some white wine. If you like bacon, put that in now.

This is good as a sauce over poached eggs or vegetables.

REMOULADE SAUCE

1 pt. mayonnaise
1 10-oz. bottle Durkee's famous sauce
1/4 cup olive oil
1 cup (8 oz.) creole mustard or poupon
1/2 cup prepared horseradish
1 cup catsup

2 TBS. wine vinegar
2 TBS. Lea & Perrins Worcestershire
   sauce
2 tsp. Louisiana hot sauce
Salt, if needed

Mix mayonnaise and Durkee sauce, pour in olive oil. and beat as if you are making mayonnaise. Add creole mustard, beat some more. Add horseradish, beat some more again. Add catsup, and yes, that's right, beat some more. Add wine vinegar, still beating. Then the Lea & Perrins, beating all the time, then the hot sauce, beating some more (this is Louisiana hot sauce made from cayenne pepper, not tabasco pepper). You may prefer ground cayenne pepper, but be careful with that.

Dis sauce is for shrimps, mostly. I want you to know dat dis taste good on most anyt'ing.

Soups and Gumbos

Seafood Soup
Squirrel and Rabbit Gumbo
Smoked Turkey Gumbo
Smoked Goose or Duck Gumbo
White Bean and Shrimp Gumbo à la Jeannine
Seafood Gumbo
Guinea Gumbo
Red Bean Gumbo
Oyster and Noodle Soup
Crawfish Chili
Oyster Chowder with Turnips

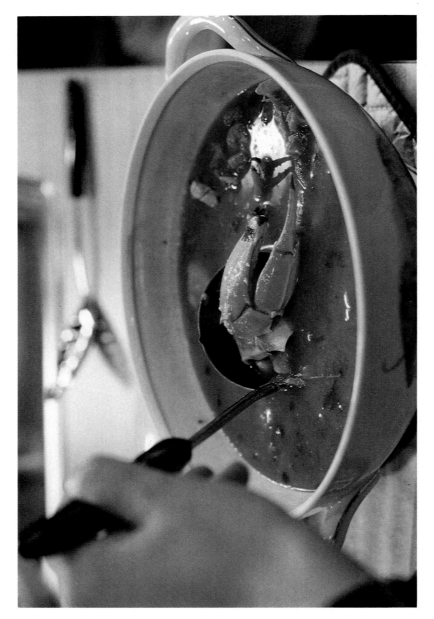

That's a crab claw, and I'm gon' open that up and eat the meat inside because O-o-o boy—it's damn good.

SEAFOOD SOUP

3 cups raw fish, boned and cubed
1 cup celery, chopped
1 cup white onions, chopped
1 cup green onions, chopped
1 cup bell pepper, chopped
1 cup carrots, chopped
1 lime or lemon, chopped fine
1 clove garlic, chopped fine

2 TBS. dried parsley (or 1 cup fresh, chopped)
2 cups each crawfish, shrimp, crab-meat, and oysters
1/2 tsp. cayenne pepper or 1 TBS. Louisiana hot sauce
Salt, to taste

Combine all of the vegetables and cover with about 1 inch water. Boil until tender. Add the fish and seafood. Bring to boil, then simmer until done.

I think it's a good idea to boil the soup for approximately 30 minutes, then simmer for 1-1/2 hours. Then you will got you some fine tastin' soup, I garontee!

SQUIRREL AND RABBIT GUMBO

1-1/2 cups onions, chopped
1/2 cup celery, chopped
1/2 cup parsley, chopped
1/2 cup bell pepper, chopped
2 tsp. garlic, chopped
2 TBS. Lea & Perrins Worcestershire sauce

4 cups dry white wine
4 cups water
Louisiana hot sauce or 1 hot pepper (cayenne)
2 lbs. meat
1 lb. andouille or smoked sausage
Flour and oil for roux

Make a very dark roux (see my recipe). Add celery, onions, and bell pepper, stirring constantly until the onions are clear. Add the garlic, parsley, water, Lea & Perrins, Louisiana hot sauce, and wine. Drop in the meat. Let cook for two or more hours.

SMOKED TURKEY GUMBO

1 smoked turkey, boned and cut up
Andouille (a lot) or smoked sausage
3 or 4 cups onions, chopped
1 cup green onions, chopped
1 TBS. garlic, chopped
1 cup bell pepper, chopped
1 cup oil or bacon drippings (maybe more than 1 cup)
2 to 4 cups plain flour
(the oil and flour are to make the roux)
1 tsp. dried mint
1 TBS. celery seed
1 cup dried parsley
4 cups dry white wine
6-1/2 drops Peychaud's bitters
2 TBS. Louisiana hot sauce
4 TBS. Lea & Perrins Worcestershire sauce
5 or 6 cups okra, sliced
Water
Salt, to taste

First, you make a dark roux about the color of a Hershey bar (see my recipe). Add onions and bell pepper. After onions are clear, add parsley and green onions and cook for a few minutes. Add a bit of cold water and stir to make a thick liquid. Add garlic and celery seed. Then add all the other ingredients and cover with water 2 to 4 inches, depending on how thick you want your gumbo. Now, if you got a lot of company or relatives, add more water. Bring to a boil, lower heat, and cook for 2 to 4 hours. Any leftover gumbo tastes better the next day, I garontee.

SMOKED GOOSE OR DUCK GUMBO

Okra
Flour
Olive oil
Bacon drippings
Deboned smoked goose or duck
Small amount of chopped celery
Chopped bell pepper
Chopped onion
Chopped parsley
Minced garlic
Lea & Perrins Worcestershire sauce
Salt
Louisiana hot sauce
Dry white wine
Water

This recipe is for smoked goose or duck; therefore the amounts are indefinite.

Make a heavy or thick roux and slowly brown until dark (see my recipe). After the roux is made, add onions, small amount of celery, and small amount of sweet or bell pepper. Then add the parsley, small amount of minced garlic, water, wine (about 1 cup, at least), okra, and other seasonings. Then add the smoked meat. Cook for several hours.

WHITE BEAN AND SHRIMP GUMBO
À LA JEANNINE

2-1/2 lbs. shrimp, peeled and deveined
Leftover white beans cooked with
   smoked sausage or andouille
1 cup cut okra
2 cups dry white wine
Louisiana hot sauce, to taste
2 TBS. Lea & Perrins Worcestershire
   sauce
1 tsp. celery seed

1 cup parsley, chopped
1 cup onions, chopped
1/2 cup bell pepper, chopped
1 tsp. garlic, chopped
1 cup green onions, chopped
Plain flour
Bacon drippings and olive oil
Salt, to taste
Water

Take the cooked beans and put through the blender to make a thick liquid. Make a roux with the flour and oil (see my recipe). When the roux is a dark chocolate color, put in onions and bell pepper. When the onion is clear, put in the parsley and green onions and continue cooking. Add a bit of cold water and stir. Then add garlic and continue cooking. Add enough water to cover everything 2 inches. Add the shrimp, wine, seasonings, and bean liquid. Cover and simmer at least 3 hours.

SEAFOOD GUMBO

1 cup olive oil
2 cups flour
3 cups onions, chopped
1 cup bell pepper, chopped
1 cup green onions, chopped
1 cup parsley, chopped
1 TBS. garlic, chopped
12 crabs, just bodies and claws (break
   bodies into halves and make sure
   the crabs are well cleaned)

2 cups oysters
1 lb. fillet of fish, cut up
2 lbs. peeled shrimp
3 tsp. Lea & Perrins Worcestershire
   sauce
2 tsp. Louisiana hot sauce
3 or 4 quarts water
2 cups dry white wine
Salt, to taste
Filé (optional)

First you make the roux (see my recipe). Add the onions and bell pepper, stirring constantly until the onions become clear. Add green onions, parsley, garlic, cold water, Lea & Perrins, salt, Louisiana hot sauce, and wine. Cook the mixture for 45 minutes, then drop in the seafood. Let cook for 2 or more hours.

Filé does not go in the pot. When you're ready to eat, sprinkle the filé over the rice and cover with steaming hot gumbo.

My young friend Tod Lobell and Pookie Babin at Pookie's Food Mart in beautiful downtown French Settlement.

GUINEA GUMBO

1 guinea hen, cut up
1-1/2 cups onions, chopped
1 tsp. garlic, minced
4 cups dry white wine
4 cups water
2 TBS. Lea & Perrins Worcestershire
    sauce

1/2 cup parsley, chopped
1 tsp. Louisiana hot sauce or 1 hot
    pepper (cayenne), chopped fine
1 cup plain flour
1 lb. andouille or smoked sausage,
    sliced
Oil or bacon drippings for roux

First make a roux (see my recipe). Brown off guinea. Add onions to roux and cook until they are clear. Then add garlic, parsley, Lea & Perrins, water, wine, and hot sauce. Then add meats. Let cook for 2 or more hours.

Dis is a special gumbo and got a taste all its own, I garontee!

RED BEAN GUMBO

Flour
Oil or bacon drippings
1 lb. red beans cooked with juice
2 lbs. andouille, sliced
2 lbs. smoked sausage, sliced
3 cups onions, chopped
2 cups bell pepper, chopped

3 cups dry white wine
Lea & Perrins Worcestershire sauce
Salt
Louisiana hot sauce
1/2 cup parsley, chopped
1 cup green onions, chopped
1 clove garlic, chopped

Make roux as always (see my recipe). Blend beans and juice in blender to make a thick liquid. Then put everything in the pot and cook. It makes a thick red gumbo.

OYSTER AND NOODLE SOUP

1/2 gallon of oysters and juice
1 cup noodles
1 cup celery, chopped
1-3/4 cups onions, chopped
1 TBS. dried parsley
2 TBS. margarine
2 TBS. olive oil

1/2 small lime or lemon, chopped fine
1 cup dry white wine
2 to 4 cups water
Salt, to taste
1/2 tsp. garlic powder
1 TBS. soy sauce
2 tsp. Louisiana hot sauce

Sauté onions and celery in margarine and oil. Add water, parsley, lemon, garlic powder, wine, soy sauce, Louisiana hot sauce, and salt. Bring to a boil, put on noodles, and let cook until tender. Add oysters and juice and cook for about thirty minutes. Be sure you have enough water so it will be soup.

CRAWFISH CHILI

2 lbs. chili meat
2 lbs. crawfish tails
1 tsp. garlic, chopped fine
2 tsp. salt
1 TBS. soy sauce
1 tsp. cayenne pepper
1 tsp. dried mint
1 TBS. dried parsley

3 TBS. chili powder
1 8-oz. can tomato sauce
1 cup dry white wine
Water
1 tsp. lemon or lime juice
1 cup onions, chopped
Bacon drippings

Brown chili meat in bacon drippings. Combine all other ingredients with meat and bring to a boil. Then simmer for a few hours.

OYSTER CHOWDER WITH TURNIPS

1 cup turnips, diced
2 TBS. olive oil
1/2 cup parsley, chopped
1 cup onions, chopped
1 TBS. Louisiana hot sauce
1 tsp. garlic, chopped

3 cups juice from oysters
1 cup dry white wine
1 TBS. soy sauce
2 TBS. salt
2 cups oysters
1 cup celery, chopped

Cook turnips in water until tender. Sauté celery, onions, and parsley in olive oil until clear or nearly done, then add garlic. Add the oyster juice and wine to the sautéed vegetables. Add the turnips with the water they are in. Bring to a boil, then cut down to a low simmer (about 170 to 175 degrees). Add the oysters, salt, soy sauce, and Louisiana hot sauce. Let the whole thing simmer for at least 6 hours—or, even better, let simmer overnight.

Breads

Cracklin' Corn Bread
Cheese Toast
Justin's Garlic Bread
Corn Bread
Whole Wheat Biscuits au Justin
Cajunized Mexican Corn Bread

This is just one step in making good cracklin' cornbread.

CRACKLIN' CORN BREAD

3 cups home- or stone-ground
  cornmeal
1 cup plain flour
1 TBS. baking powder
Soda, a pinch

Buttermilk, just enough so that mix
  will be thick but still pour
Cracklin's, crumbled up
2 TBS. cooking oil, heated
3 or 2 eggs

Preheat oven to 400 degrees. Mix all ingredients except oil. Put cooking oil in iron skillet that will be used to bake corn bread. Heat oil in skillet and pour into mixture as the last ingredient in mixture. Pour mixture back into iron skillet in which oil was heated. Bake in preheated oven. When browned, flip corn bread over. Turn off oven and put skillet with corn bread back in oven for a few minutes.

Cracklin's are pork rinds that are made when lard is rendered.

CHEESE TOAST

Yellow cheddar cheese
Swiss cheese
Creole or Poupon mustard

Bread, or bagels, or buns, or biscuits,
  or toast

You can toast one side, but it is not necessary. Spread one side of bread with mustard. Slice cheese and arrange on top of mustard. Run under broiler until cheese melts. Serve immediately.

You most probably will have to stand guard at the oven door. That cheese melts so fast that if you try to do anything else, you will be sorry.

JUSTIN'S GARLIC BREAD

Bread, preferably Italian twist or
  French, sliced lengthwise
Margarine or butter, spread
  generously on bread
Garlic powder, sprinkled on margarine

Parmesan or Romano cheese,
  sprinkled on butter
Dried parsley, sprinkled over cheese
Black pepper, sprinkled over parsley

Bake a little first to melt cheese, then toast with the broiler. Serve immediately.

CORN BREAD

2 cups, home- or stone-ground
   cornmeal
1 tsp. salt
1 cup plain flour

1/2 tsp. baking soda
2 eggs
1-1/2 to 2 cups buttermilk
2-1/2 TBS. shortening

Mix dry ingredients together well. Heat shortening in skillet. (Use a large skillet or two small ones.) Beat eggs really well. Pour buttermilk into beaten eggs. Pour this mixture into dry ingredients and mix well. If necessary, add more buttermilk. Be careful not to make mixture runny. Pour shortening in this batter. Beat hell out of it.

Pour back into hot skillet. Bake in 400-degree oven until well browned. Flip bread over in skillet to sweat it. Turn oven off and put bread back into it for a few minutes.

WHOLE WHEAT BISCUITS AU JUSTIN

1 cup plain white flour
1 cup plain whole wheat flour
1/2 tsp. salt
3 TBS. shortening

1/2 tsp. soda
1 cup buttermilk
3 tsp. baking powder

Mix flour, soda, and baking powder and salt well. Cut in shortening. Pour in buttermilk; mix. Flour hands and roll out dough. Cut biscuits and place on well-greased cookie sheets. Bake in 400-degree oven until brown.

CAJUNIZED MEXICAN CORN BREAD

2 cups home- or stone-ground
   cornmeal
1 cup plain flour
3 tsp. baking powder
1-1/2 tsp. salt
1/4 tsp. soda
3 TBS. bacon drippings or shortening
3 eggs

1 cup whole kernel corn
1 cup cheddar cheese, grated
1 TBS. hot pepper, chopped,
   preferably fresh cayenne or
   jalapeño
2 TBS. bell pepper, chopped
2 TBS. onions, chopped fine
1 to 2 cups buttermilk

Use a big skillet or 2 small ones. Mix dry ingredients really well. Heat bacon drippings or shortening in skillet. Add cheese, peppers, and onions to dry ingredients and mix well. Beat hell out of eggs. Pour 1/2 buttermilk into eggs and mix well. Then pour eggs into dry mixture and beat well. Add rest of buttermilk as needed. Pour shortening from skillet and beat. Pour batter into skillet and bake at 350 degrees until browned. Flip corn bread over in skillet. Turn oven off and put bread back in oven for a few minutes.

Casseroles

Corn Bread Dressing
Rice Dressing
Fillet of Fish and Rice Casserole
Rice–Tuna Casserole
Macaroni and Crawfish and Cheese Casserole
Eggplant Crawfish Casserole
Turnip Casserole with Shrimp
Crawfish and Turnip Casserole
Rice and Crawfish Casserole
Squash–Shrimp Casserole
Squash–Tuna Casserole
Rice au Gratin
Macaroni or Spaghetti and Cheese

This is Gilbert Matherne, one of my chief testers when we cook something. He's chief of police in French Settlement.

Here are No. 1 and No. 2 tasters and testers, Dr. Charles Johnson and Lisa Cook. Doc is a for real, for true gourmet-gourmand, and Lisa is a real good helper for him.

CORN BREAD DRESSING

6 eggs, well beaten
1 pan corn bread
2 cups celery, chopped fine
6 cups onions, chopped fine
12 slices toast, crumbled
1 tsp. dried mint, crushed

Salt and red pepper, to taste
10 cups hot chicken or turkey stock
(Make your stock from the chopped fine giblets)
Enough boiling water to make heavy mixture

Crumble bread and toast. Add all ingredients together. Use some of this and stuff your turkey or chicken, including the craw. Sew the bird together. Do not over-stuff.

The rest of the stuffing is to be placed in a roaster and baked at 325 degrees until done. This should take about 2 hours. You can check it by inserting a broomstraw. If it comes out clean, the dressing is done.

RICE DRESSING

6 cups rice, cooked
1 cup onions, chopped
1 cup green onions, chopped
1 cup parsley or 1/2 cup dried parsley
1/2 cup celery, chopped
1/2 cup bell pepper, chopped
1 8-oz. can stems and pieces mushrooms
6 eggs, beaten
1 tsp. garlic, chopped

Salt, to taste
3 TBS. bacon drippings
2 cups giblets and liver (turkey or chicken)
2 cups dry white wine
2 TBS. Lea & Perrins Worcestershire sauce
1 tsp. dried mint (crushed fine)
1 TBS. Louisiana hot sauce or 1 tsp. ground cayenne pepper

Boil giblets and liver in wine and 2 cups water. Sauté onions, green onions, celery, bell pepper, and parsley in bacon drippings until onions are clear. When juicy enough, add garlic. Chop giblets and liver up fine. Blend all ingredients together and then add beaten eggs. Stuff the bird with part of this and place the rest in a roaster and bake at 350 degrees for 1 hour.

FILLET OF FISH AND RICE CASSEROLE

1/2 cup onions, chopped
1/4 cup bell pepper, chopped
1/4 cup dried parsley
1/2 cup water
1 cup dry white wine
1 tsp. garlic, chopped
6 cups rice, cooked
3 tsp. butter-flavored salt

4 cups fish fillets, cut up
2 tsp. Louisiana hot sauce
1 TBS. Lea & Perrins Worcestershire
  sauce
6 drops Peychaud's bitters
Pimento, chopped
Romano cheese, grated

Cook onions, peppers, garlic, and parsley in the water and wine until tender. Mix raw fish, cooked rice, and all other ingredients (except the Romano cheese) and put in a greased casserole. Top with cheese and bake in 325-degree oven for 1 hour.

Dis will not serve as many as you t'ink. It are too good.

RICE–TUNA CASSEROLE

1 6-oz. can tuna
1 4-oz. can mushrooms
3 cups rice, cooked
1 tsp. onion powder
1/2 tsp. garlic powder
1/4 tsp. celery seed
6 drops Peychaud's bitters
1/2 tsp. lemon pepper
1/4 tsp. butter-flavored salt

1 tsp. Louisiana hot sauce
2 tsp. Lea & Perrins Worcestershire
  sauce
6 eggs, beaten
1 cup dry white wine
1 TBS. pimento, chopped
1/2 tsp. dried mint, crushed
Romano cheese

Beat the wine and eggs together with seasonings. Add liquids to tuna and rice, mushrooms and pimentos, and cheese. Mix together and put in a greased casserole dish. Bake at 325 degrees for 1 hour.

MACARONI AND CRAWFISH AND CHEESE CASSEROLE

━━━━◆━━━━

2 lbs. crawfish tails
1 lb. fresh mushrooms
2 cups cheddar cheese, grated
1 cup swiss cheese, grated
1/2 cup Romano cheese, grated
2 cups onions, chopped
1 TBS. garlic, chopped
6 eggs, beaten really well
1 lb. elbow macaroni, almost cooked

Salt, to taste
1 10-oz. can mushroom gravy
Louisiana hot sauce or cayenne
 pepper, to taste
1 TBS. Lea & Perrins Worcestershire
 sauce
2 cups seasoned bread crumbs
1 TBS. dried parsley

Mix crawfish, mushrooms, cheese, parsley, onions, garlic, and macaroni really well.

In a separate bowl, beat six eggs and add mushroom gravy, wine, and seasonings. Pour into crawfish mixture and mix well. Put in casserole and top with bread crumbs. Cover and cook in 350-degree oven for 1 to 1-1/2 hours.

EGGPLANT CRAWFISH CASSEROLE

━━━━◆━━━━

6 medium-large eggplants, peeled and
 cubed
1-1/2 cups onions, chopped
1/2 cup parsley, chopped
2 tsp. garlic, chopped
2 lbs. crawfish tails
1 cup green onions, chopped
2 TBS. bacon drippings, to sauté
 onions and parsley
2 TBS. soy sauce

Salt, to taste
2 tsp. Louisiana hot sauce
Olive oil, enough to grease bottom and
 sides of casserole
1 cup dry white wine
2 cups seasoned bread crumbs
4 eggs, beaten
1 TBS. Lea & Perrins Worcestershire
 sauce

Parboil eggplants until soft, then drain. Sauté onions and parsley. Combine everything in a big bowl and mix well. Sprinkle bread crumbs on top and bake in a greased casserole for 1 hour at 325 degrees.

Feeds 6 Cajuns or 12 normal peoples, unless dey are gourmands.

Ed Wall, Jerry Cupit and I have been quail hunting. Some of those quail were too dumb to know they were dead, and kept on flying.

TURNIP CASSEROLE WITH SHRIMP

10 cups turnips, cooked and mashed
1 cup green onions, chopped
1/2 lb. bacon, diced
1/2 cup dried parsley
Salt, to taste
2 cups seasoned bread crumbs
1 TBS. Lea & Perrins Worcestershire
    sauce

1/2 tsp. Louisiana hot sauce
1 cup dry white wine
1/2 tsp. garlic powder
1 cup cheddar cheese, grated
2 cups shrimp or crawfish, cut up
1 cup fillet of fish, chopped
4 eggs, beaten

Layer turnips, cheese, shrimp (or crawfish), fish, onions, bacon, and bread crumbs. Make 2 layers. Beat eggs and blend with rest of ingredients. Pour this mixture over the layers in the dish. Bake at 350 degrees for about 1 hour.

WHO-O-O-O-O Boy—you' taste bud goin' to go into full bloom on dis.

CRAWFISH AND TURNIP CASSEROLE

2 to 4 lbs. crawfish
2 to 4 cups turnips
1 to 2 cups dry white wine
2 TBS. dried parsley
Salt, to taste
2 tsp. Louisiana hot sauce
6 drops Peychaud's bitters
1-1/2 cups onions, chopped
1 tsp. garlic, chopped

Olive oil to grease casserole
2 TBS. soy sauce
1 to 2 cups mushrooms, chopped
    (fresh or canned)
1/2 to 1/4 cup lime, chopped
2 TBS. margarine, melted
1 or 2 TBS. Lea & Perrins
    Worcestershire sauce

Mix all ingredients in a big bowl until well blended. Put in greased casserole dishes and bake at 325 degrees for 1-1/2 to 2 hours.

Serves 8 Cajuns or 16 other peoples. You may substitute shrimp for crawfish.

RICE AND CRAWFISH CASSEROLE

1/2 cup bell pepper, chopped
1/2 cup celery, chopped
1 heaping cup green onions, chopped
1/2 cup parsley, chopped
2 cups crawfish tails
2 cups mushrooms (fresh or canned)
2 TBS. olive oil to sauté first 4
    ingredients

4 cups rice, cooked
1 tsp. garlic, chopped
6 eggs, beaten
1 cup dry white wine
2 tsp. Louisiana hot sauce
1 TBS. soy sauce
2 tsp. salt

Sauté onions, pepper, celery, and parsley. Beat together last 5 ingredients. Combine all ingredients in a big bowl. Pour liquid mixture over all. Bake in a greased, covered casserole in a 325-degree oven for 1 hour.

It won't taste as good, but you can substitute shrimp for crawfish.

SQUASH-SHRIMP CASSEROLE

8 cups squash, chopped
3 cups onions, chopped
1 cup bell pepper, chopped
1 cup dried shrimp
1 big clove garlic, minced
Salt
1 cup dry white wine

Red cayenne pepper
Bread crumbs
Parmesan cheese
1 large banana pepper, chopped
  (or pickled pepper)
3 eggs, beaten well
2 TBS. olive oil

Put olive oil in a large pot. Sauté the onions, hot pepper, and bell pepper until clear. Add the squash and 1 cup wine. Cook until tender, then stir in the shrimp and garlic, and cook 10 minutes. Beat the eggs and fold into the squash mixture.

Turn the mixture into a deep casserole dish. Top with bread crumbs and Parmesan cheese. Bake at 325 degrees for 1 hour or until brown.

SQUASH–TUNA CASSEROLE

8 to 10 cups squash, chopped
2 cups onions, chopped
1/4 cup green onions, chopped
1/2 cup bell pepper, chopped
1 cup dry white wine
1/2 to 1 cup fresh mushrooms
2 TBS. Lea & Perrins Worcestershire
  sauce
2 tsp. Louisiana hot sauce, or 1/4 tsp.
  cayenne pepper

Salt
1 cup water
2 tsp. garlic, chopped
1 tsp. dried mint
2 cups tuna, drained
2 TBS. bacon drippings
Seasoned bread crumbs

In bacon drippings, sauté onions and bell pepper until clear. Add wine and water and other seasonings, including garlic. Don't add bread crumbs. Add all the rest and cook on top of the stove until tender. Top with bread crumbs and bake at 325 degrees for 1 hour in a greased casserole.

RICE AU GRATIN

4 cups rice, cooked
3/4 cup olives with pimento, sliced
1 cup dry white wine
4 eggs, beaten well
3-1/2 cups cheese (three kinds:
    cheddar, swiss, Romano), all grated

1 TBS. olive oil
1 tsp. Louisiana hot sauce
1 TBS. soy sauce
Salt, to taste (not much)
2 cups mushrooms, chopped

Beat together eggs, wine, hot sauce, soy sauce, and salt.

Grease casserole with olive oil. Using half of the rice, cover bottom really well. Cover rice with mushrooms and olives. Layer 1-1/2 to 2 cups of grated cheeses (mixed). Then layer rice. Then another layer of grated cheeses. Add egg mixture. Bake at 325 degrees for about 30 to 45 minutes.

MACARONI OR SPAGHETTI AND CHEESE

1 lb. pasta, cooked and cooled
6 eggs (at least), beaten
2 cups dry white wine
1 cup onions, chopped
1 tsp. Louisiana hot sauce
Salt, to taste

2 TBS. Lea & Perrins Worcestershire
    sauce
1 cup smoked sausage, sliced
1 cup mushrooms, sliced
4 cups and more grated cheeses, swiss,
    cheddar, and Romano, mixed

Grease casserole with olive oil. Beat eggs, adding wine, then all seasonings to liquid. Mix all ingredients well. Put in casserole and top with yellow cheese. Bake at 325 degrees for about 1 hour.

Feeds 6 Cajuns or 14 regular peoples with some left over for the next day.
This tastes some good cold sliced with a bunch of mayonnaise and Louisiana hot sauce on top as a salad.

Here's a whole P-I-G hog. We goin' to cook him in a Cajun microwave.

Meats

Sausage Jambalaya
Pork Jambalaya
Leftover Lamb Meat Sauce
Meat Sauce
Cajunized Oriental Pork Chops
Baked/Broiled Pork Chops with Mint
12-Pound Canned Ham
Baked Pork Ribs

SAUSAGE JAMBALAYA

3 cups rice, long grain
2 lbs. smoked sausage or andouille,
   sliced thick
2 8-oz. cans tomato sauce
3 cups onions, chopped
2 cups bell pepper, chopped
1 tsp. garlic, minced

1/4 cup parsley, chopped
Louisiana hot sauce
Salt to taste
Olive oil to sauté onion
2 cups dry white wine
Water

Sauté onions and bell pepper in olive oil and cook until onions are clear. Add garlic, parsley, tomato sauce, and wine. Then add rice. Add smoked sausage or andouille and enough water to cover about 1 inch above ingredients. Cook on medium high heat until most of the juice is gone. Then cover and simmer 1 hour. This makes a red jambalaya.

Don't let anyone try to look—chop at their hands if they start to do that.

PORK JAMBALAYA

3 cups long-grain rice
2-1/2 lbs. pork cut in chunks
3 cups onions, chopped
1 tsp. garlic, chopped
2 TBS. parsley, chopped
1 TBS. celery, chopped

Salt, to taste
Cayenne pepper, to taste
1 cup oil
1 cup dry white wine
3 cups water

First brown pork. Sauté onions and bell pepper in oil. Add other seasonings, wine, and water, then add rice. Have enough water to cover ingredients about 1 inch. Cook on medium heat until most of the juice is gone. Then cover and simmer 1 hour. Don't remove the cover until the hour is past.

LEFTOVER LAMB MEAT SAUCE

Grind leftover lamb in food processor or meat grinder.

Onions, chopped
Garlic, chopped
Celery, chopped (little of this)
Bell pepper, chopped (little of this)
Louisiana hot sauce

Salt, to taste
Lea & Perrins Worcestershire sauce
   or soy sauce
Small amount of dry white wine

Sauté onions, celery, and bell pepper in oleo or bacon drippings (just a small amount). Add garlic when onions become clear, and add rest of ingredients and cook over low heat for two hours. Notice there are no measurements. Everything depend on how much lamb is leftover.

MEAT SAUCE

2 lbs. ground chuck
1 cup onions, chopped
1/2 cup bell pepper, chopped
1 tsp. celery seed
1 tsp. dried mint (crushed)
1 8-oz. can mushrooms (stems and
   pieces)
Olive oil, enough to sauté onions, bell
   pepper, and meat

8 drops Peychaud's bitters
2 8-oz. cans tomato sauce
2 cups dry red wine
2 tsp. salt
3 TBS. Lea & Perrins Worcestershire
   sauce
2 tsp. Louisiana hot sauce
2 tsp. garlic, chopped

Sauté meat with just enough oil until every grain of meat stands apart—like sawdust. Sauté onions and bell pepper separately until they are clear and tender. Put all ingredients together and bring to a boil. Simmer for 2 to 3 hours. Serves about 6, depending on who is eating. Serve with spaghetti.

Bill Holford, my partner in the recording business, and Bob Ruby, who has a very fine restaurant in Houston. If you think we're talking about food, you're right.

You see everybody laughing there. The pig that was getting cut up must have said something funny, hanh. That's Mrs. Yvonne Lobell, Travis Lobell with the knife, Huntley Hitchinson and me.

CAJUNIZED ORIENTAL PORK CHOPS

6 thick pork chops
Salt and red cayenne pepper
1-1/2 cups dry white wine
1 cup bell pepper, chopped

1 cup onions, chopped
1 clove garlic, chopped
3 TBS. soy sauce
1 can (15 oz.) pineapple chunks

Salt and red pepper the chops. Brown them slowly in a skillet. Add wine, bell pepper, onion, and garlic. Cover and simmer for 25 to 30 minutes. Remove pork chops, being sure to keep them warm.

Add the soy sauce and syrup from the pineapple. Stir and simmer until more or less thick. Add the pineapple chunks and bring to a boil. Serve over pork chops and hot cooked rice. Serves six.

BAKED/BROILED PORK CHOPS WITH MINT

Pork chops
Red cayenne pepper
Salt

Lea & Perrins Worcestershire sauce
Dried mint
White wine (small amount)

Sprinkle chops with salt, red cayenne pepper, and mint. Put on top of a broiler pan. Pour wine with Lea & Perrins in bottom of broiler pan. Bake 30 minutes at 325 degrees, then turn and broil.

12-POUND CANNED HAM

1 big ham already cooked
Place in foil (in a pan) to cover
   completely
1 cup honey
1/2 cup mustard

2 TBS. steak sauce
1 16-oz. can sliced pineapple (reserve
   juice)
Cloves

Use toothpicks to arrange pineapple slices on ham top and sides. Push whole cloves into meat. Mix honey, mustard, steak sauce, and juice from pineapple. Pour this over ham. Bake at 325 degrees for 1 hour or until heated through.

This is an easy-cook ham for holidays or funerals.

BAKED PORK RIBS

Pork ribs
Red cayenne pepper
Salt

Mint
1/2 cup dry white wine

Salt and pepper pork ribs. Sprinkle crushed mint on ribs. Place on a broiler pan that has holes in the top. Pour wine in bottom of broiler pan. Bake at 325 degrees until ribs separate from meat. Use as many ribs as will cover broiler pan. Turn twice. Ribs will be juicy but not as greasy as usual.

Seafood

Leftover White Beans with Crawfish or Shrimp
Oyster Jambalaya
Shrimp Sauce Piquante
Yeola's Crawfish Bisque
Broiled Oysters
Baked Fish in an Open Pan
Barbecued Oysters
Soft-Shelled Crabs
Fish Courtbouillon au Justin
Boiled Shrimp
Baked Fish
Crawfish Sauté au Justin
Broiled Frog Legs
Eggplant with Shrimp and Crab and Fish
Catfish with Cornbread Stuffing
Dishwasher Fish
Wayne Levi's Genuine Original Boiled Crawfish

This catfish weighed 27 pounds. We fixin' to bake him with lemon butter sauce.

LEFTOVER WHITE BEANS WITH CRAWFISH OR SHRIMP

1 lb. crawfish tails
Leftover beans

2 or 3 slices of crisp fried bacon,
   crumbled
Onions, chopped fine

Put crawfish or shrimp into pot with leftover beans and the bacon. Bring to a boil and then turn heat down to low. Bubble boil for 30 minutes. Serve in bowl with onions added.

OYSTER JAMBALAYA

1 cup onions, chopped
1/2 cup bell pepper, chopped
1 cup mushrooms, sliced
1 quart oysters with juice
3 cups rice
1 tsp. garlic, chopped
1/2 TBS. parsley, chopped

1 4-oz. can tomato sauce
1 TBS. bacon drippings
1 TBS. olive oil
1 cup dry white wine
1 TBS. Louisiana hot sauce
1 TBS. Kitchen Bouquet, optional
Water

Sauté onions and bell pepper in olive oil and bacon drippings. Add mushrooms and a little water, then add garlic and parsley. Add tomato sauce, wine, Louisiana hot sauce and Kitchen Bouquet, and then add rice. Add oysters with their juice, having liquid cover other ingredients about 1 inch. Cook on medium high heat until most of the juice is gone. Then cover and simmer 1 hour.

Don't let anyone raise the lid to look—chop at their hands if they start to do that.

SHRIMP SAUCE PIQUANTE

4 lbs. jumbo shrimp, peeled
2 cups onions, chopped
1 cup green onions, chopped
3/4 cup bell pepper, chopped
1/2 cup celery, chopped
4 8-oz. cans tomato sauce
1 tsp. garlic, chopped
1 lemon, chopped fine

1 cup plain flour
1/2 cup olive oil or bacon drippings
2 cups dry white wine
Red cayenne pepper or Louisiana hot
   sauce
6 drops Peychaud's bitters
Lea & Perrins Worcestershire sauce,
   to taste

Make a dark roux with the flour and olive oil (see my recipe). Add onions, pepper, and celery. Cook until the vegetables are clear. Add green onions and parsley, and continue cooking. Stir in the water, tomato sauce, garlic, hot sauce, Lea & Perrins, and salt. Add the shrimp. Bring to a boil and let simmer for about 2 hours. We sometimes cook it longer than 2 hours. Serve over spaghetti or rice.

YEOLA'S CRAWFISH BISQUE

Put 40 pounds of crawfish in a large tub and sprinkle with enough salt to make a strong brine. Let soak to purge. Rinse well.

Scald and clean the crawfish. Separate the head from the body, cleaning the head so that it is hollow. After the heads have been cleaned, put them in a pot with two tablespoons baking soda and boil until they are clean all the way plum. Rinse. This is the part that is stuffed.

STUFFING FOR CRAWFISH HEADS

3 lbs. crawfish tails
2 cups seasoned bread crumbs
2 large onions
3 celery sticks
1 large bell pepper, cleaned
1 cup green onions, chopped

1/2 cup parsley, chopped
1 cup Pet evaporated milk
3 eggs
1 TBS. salt
1 TBS. red cayenne pepper

Clean about 150 heads and boil in a large pot with two tablespoons baking soda.

Grind crawfish tails, onions, celery, and bell pepper. In a large bowl mix with remaining ingredients and push stuffing into heads. Roll the stuffed part in flour and fry just enough to set stuffing.

GRAVY FOR HEADS

1 cup flour
1/2 cup oil
2 large onions, chopped
3 celery sticks, chopped
1 large bell pepper, chopped
3/4 cup green onions, chopped
1/2 cup parsley, chopped

1 can Ro-tel
1 can tomato sauce (8 oz.)
1 TBS. crab boil (liquid)
3 cloves garlic, chopped
Salt and red pepper, to taste
2 quarts water

Make a roux (see my recipe). When roux is a dark chocolate color, add onions, celery, bell pepper, and garlic. Simmer on low heat until onions are clear. Add Ro-tel, tomato sauce, and liquid crab boil. Add 1 quart water. Cook slowly about 30 minutes. Add crawfish tails, green onions, and parsley. Add another quart of water. Cook some more. Put in the stuffed heads, and salt and red pepper to taste. Let simmer about 45 minutes. Makes about 2 gallons and 150 heads.

Some peoples t'ink that this is an awful lot of trouble to make a bisque and I want to tole you, it sure as hell is. Dat's why I don't make it. I go to my good friends Yeola and Dallas Jones' house when I want to have de best bisque in the world.

BROILED OYSTERS

Large oysters
Pam
Salt

Lemon pepper seasoning
Butter-flavored salt
Dry white wine

Spray a baking pan with Pam. Sprinkle salt, butter-flavored salt, and lemon pepper over each oyster. Put a little wine on the bottom of the pan to use for basting. Add oysters and broil until done. Eat as soon as they come out of the oven.

BAKED FISH IN AN OPEN PAN

3 to 4 lb. fish (larger if you are lucky)
1 lb. margarine
1/4 cup lemon juice
1/4 cup lime juice
Salt, to taste

2 TBS. Lea & Perrins Worcestershire
    sauce or soy sauce
2 tsp. Louisiana hot sauce
6 drops Peychaud's bitters

Combine melted margarine with all ingredients. Pour over fish and bake at 325 degrees for about 30 minutes. Baste frequently and test flesh with fork. The testing with a fork will tell you if you got a done fish. If it flakes easily, it's done.

BARBECUED OYSTERS

4 doz. oysters
1/2 cup chili powder
1/2 cup plain flour
1 tsp. cayenne pepper

1 tsp. garlic powder
1 TBS. salt
1 tsp. hickory-smoked salt

Put the dry ingredients in a heavy paper bag and shake real well. Add oysters one at a time and shake. Fry in deep hot fat (about 360 to 365 degrees) until done.

I've got to get my hot pepper plants, and my friend Dale Zuelke here guaranteed that they'll be as hot as 12 yards of you know where.

Dallas Jones keeps my stoves and refrigerators and freezers going all the time, so I've always got something good to cook. You'll find out about his wife Yeola in her crawfish bisque recipe.

SOFT-SHELLED CRABS

1 doz. crabs
Olive oil to grease broiler pan
Lemon-butter sauce
   1 lb. butter or margarine
   1 TBS. soy sauce
   1 TBS. Lea & Perrins
     Worcestershire sauce

1 tsp. Louisiana hot sauce
2 lemons, squeezed
2 limes, squeezed
1 TBS. parsley, chopped
Salt, to taste

Clean crabs and broil, turning once. Pour sauce over them when done. When done means when tender. Use kitchen fork to test for tender.

FISH COURTBOUILLON AU JUSTIN

3 cups onions, chopped
2 cups celery, chopped
1 cup bell pepper, chopped
1/2 cup parsley, chopped
2 cups green onions, chopped
1 TBS. garlic, chopped
5 or 6 cups fish, boned and skinned in
   big pieces
2 TBS. olive oil
2 cups carrots, grated

1/4 cup lemon, chopped fine
2 cups dry white wine
8 cups water
1 TBS. soy sauce
1 TBS. Lea & Perrins Worcestershire
   sauce
2 tsp. Louisiana hot sauce
1/4 tsp. Peychaud's bitters
3 to 4 tsp. salt

In a large heavy pot, sauté onions, celery, and bell pepper in olive oil until clear. Add parsley, green onions, garlic, and carrots and simmer for about 15 minutes. Pour in lemon, wine, fish, and the remainder of the ingredients.

Bring to a boil, and let cook over low heat (nearly simmer) for 3 to 4 hours. Do not stir. This can be made with a light roux, also, too.

BOILED SHRIMP

Cayenne pepper to taste
6 lemons, quartered
1 TBS. celery seed
1 TBS. mustard seed
1 tsp. dill seed
3 cups dry white wine

3 TBS. Lea & Perrins Worcestershire
  sauce
1 tsp. dried mint, crushed
Water
1/2 cup salt (real salty)
Shrimp, raw

Put all seasonings in enough water to cover shrimp. Amount of seasoning depends on the amount of shrimp to be boiled. Bring to a hard boil for about 10 minutes. Add shrimp and boil for about 5 to 10 minutes until shell seems to separate from flesh. *DO NOT OVER COOK!*

For 5 lbs. of shrimp, use the above amounts of ingredients.

BAKED FISH

A big fish, boned if possible
1 lb. butter or margarine
2 lemons, squeezed
2 limes, squeezed
Salt, to taste

Red cayenne pepper, to taste
1 TBS. soy sauce
1 TBS. Lea & Perrins Worcestershire
  sauce
1 TBS. parsley, chopped

Bake in an open pan—a deep one. Place fish in open pan and pat salt and red pepper into it. For lemon butter sauce, heat butter or margarine (do not boil) and add lime juice, lemon juice, soy sauce, and Lea & Perrins and parsley to this. Pour over fish and bake at 325 degrees. Check fish with fork to see if it is done. Should be done in about 20 to 30 minutes.

CRAWFISH SAUTÉ AU JUSTIN

2 TBS. margarine
1/2 cup mushrooms, chopped
1 lime, chopped fine
4 lbs. crawfish
3 TBS. soy sauce
4 cups dry white wine

4 tsp. Louisiana hot sauce
1 tsp. onion powder
1/4 tsp. garlic powder
6 drops Peychaud's bitters
1 TBS. salt

Sauté mushrooms in margarine, add wine, lime, and crawfish and other seasonings. Bring mixture to a boil. Simmer 1 hour.

Serve over rice or just plain serve it.

BROILED FROG LEGS

1 doz. frog legs
1 lb. butter or margarine
1 TBS. soy sauce
1 TBS. Lea & Perrins Worcestershire
  sauce

Salt to taste
1 tsp. Louisiana hot sauce
2 lemons, squeezed
2 limes, squeezed
1 TBS. parsley, chopped

Make lemon butter sauce (see Baked Fish). Broil frog legs plain. Pour sauce over them when they are done.

Dey (de frog leg) ain't goin' to jump out of de oven, no.

EGGPLANT WITH SHRIMP AND
CRAB AND FISH

2 lbs. of raw shrimp, crabmeat, or raw
  fish, or whatever you like
3 large eggplants, peeled and cubed
1 cup onions, chopped
1/2 cup parsley, chopped
1 tsp. dried mint, chopped
1 tsp. garlic, minced
1/2 cup green onions, chopped
1 TBS. Lea & Perrins Worcestershire
  sauce

3 TBS. bacon drippings to sauté
  onions
1 TBS. soy sauce
2 tsp. Louisiana hot sauce
Olive oil to grease dish
2 cups seasoned bread crumbs
4 eggs, beaten
Salt

Parboil eggplant until soft, then drain. Sauté onions, mix all other ingredients except bread crumbs together in a large bowl, and put in a greased casserole. Put bread crumbs on top and bake at 325 degrees for 1 hour.

Dis will feed some gourmets and maybe three or two gourmands.

You see Wayne Levi here. He knows more about crawfish than crawfish do theyselves. I garontee.

CATFISH WITH CORN BREAD STUFFING

1 large catfish, remove the eyes
Corn Bread Stuffing:

    6 slices toast, crumbled
    3 cups onions, chopped
    1 cup celery, chopped fine
    1 cup parsley, chopped

1 small pan corn bread, crumbled
Salt and red pepper
5 cups hot fish stock (I usually cut
    off the head and boil it to make
    my stock)

Mix all of the above ingredients.

Grease catfish with olive oil inside and outside. Pat on red cayenne pepper and salt. Stuff cavity with dressing.

You can cook any stuffing that you can't get into the cavity in a deep baking pan or roaster.

This are good an' mos' peoples never t'ink to did dis kine of t'ing.

DISHWASHER FISH

1 lb. fish fillets
1/4 lb. butter, melted
1 TBS. lemon juice

Salt, to taste
Red cayenne pepper, to taste

Put all ingredients in a small deep aluminum foil pan. Cover tight, tight with aluminum foil. Set the dishwasher to the regular cycle and load with dirty dishes. Place the pan where it will not be upset. Turn on dishwasher.

You got to have a good hot water heater for this dish. I mean, the water in your house got to get hot, hot, hot.

WAYNE LEVI'S GENUINE
ORIGINAL BOILED CRAWFISH

50 lbs. live crawfish
4 3-oz. packages Zatarain's dry crab
   boil, broken up
1/2 cup Zatarain's liquid crab boil

2-1/2 lbs. iodized salt
1/2 lb. ground cayenne pepper
1 tsp. granulated garlic

Put all seasonings in a big pot that will hold 50 pounds of crawfish. Fill half full of cold water. Bring water with seasonings to a rolling boil.

Wash crawfish in cold water (a hose works well for this), and pick out the dead ones. Put crawfish in the pot and bring them barely back to a boil. It will have a red foam on top.

Turn off fire. Then, to cool pot down, spray the top of the crawfish and sides of the pot with cold water. Do not run cold water over crawfish.

Leave crawfish in pot for thirty minutes and stir every 5 minutes.

After 30 minutes, take the crawfish out of the pot. Sit down and have a good time.

Fowl and Eggs

Crawfish Omelet
Baked Chicken What-the-Hell
Baked Chicken—Cut Up
Broiled Chicken
Crème de Menthe and Onion Omelet
Leftover Pasta and Eggs
Ain't No Quiche
Eggs Jambalaya
Thanksgiving Leftover Turkey Sauce Piquant

I've got a real helper named Ricky French helping me stuff the turkey with rice dressing. You can see he got both eyes, his nose, and his mouth as well as both hands helping me do that.

CRAWFISH OMELET

1 cup cleaned crawfish tails (save the fat from the tails)
1/2 cup onions, chopped

Salt and red pepper, to taste
2 TBS. margarine or butter
6 eggs

Sauté onions in margarine until clear. Add crawfish and simmer until crawfish are tender or nearly done.

Beat eggs well. Put enough butter or margarine in frying pan to cook eggs (about 2 teaspoons). Cook and fold in crawfish and cook until firm. This is a well done omelet.

BAKED CHICKEN WHAT-THE-HELL

Rick ✗✗✗ +
Laurie ✗✗✗✗
extremely different
not spicy, but the
mint is tremendous

2 fryers, cut up
2 cups burgundy wine
Salt
Cayenne pepper
2 TBS. Lea & Perrins Worcestershire sauce
A little olive oil to spread on chicken

Sprinkle of dried mint
Sprinkle of dried parsley
1 tsp. onion powder
1/2 tsp. garlic powder
1 cup pecans, crumbled
1-1/2 cups fresh mushrooms, sliced

Put chicken in baking pan. Pat salt and cayenne pepper on it after pouring a little olive oil on each piece of chicken. Sprinkle mint, parsley, pecans, and mushrooms on chicken. Mix wine, Lea & Perrins, onion powder, and garlic powder and pour down the side of the pan. Cover with foil. Bake at 325 degrees for 1 hour and 45 minutes to 2 hours. Take foil off for last few minutes.

Serves 6 to 8, dependin' on who it is and what kine of hunger is on 'em.

BAKED CHICKEN—CUT UP

1 fryer, cut up
Red cayenne pepper
Salt

Dried mint
2 cups dry white wine
Broiler pan with holes and bottom pan

Pat mint, salt, and pepper on chicken. Place on top of broiler pan. Pour wine in bottom pan. Bake in 325 degree oven. Should be cooked in about 30 minutes, maybe less. Look at it and if it is browned and starting to show bone away from flesh, it is done.

BROILED CHICKEN

1 fryer, cut in half
1-1/2 cups dry white wine
Red cayenne pepper
Olive oil

Soy sauce
1 cup fresh mushrooms, sliced
Pam
3/4 cup water

Spray pan with Pam. Rub olive oil into chicken, and place in pan. Sprinkle red pepper on chicken and mushrooms. Sprinkle soy sauce on chicken generously. Pour wine in pan (not on chicken). Add about 3/4 cup of water. Broil and keep an eye on it. Turn chicken at least twice.

CRÈME DE MENTHE AND ONION OMELET

1/4 cup onions, chopped
1/4 cup crème de menthe
4 eggs, beaten

Salt, to taste
Louisiana hot sauce, to taste

Marinate onions overnight in crème de menthe. Drain. Beat eggs, add salt and hot sauce. Then cook as you would a regular omelet, adding onions last.

LEFTOVER PASTA AND EGGS

**** !
Do again

Bacon drippings or oleo margarine
Pasta—as much as you have
Onion powder
Garlic powder

Romano cheese, grated
Louisiana hot sauce
Eggs

Naturally there are no measures on this leftover dish. Place drippings or oleo in frying pan or skillet. Add garlic powder and onion powder. On low heat, add pasta, cheese, and hot sauce, stirring constantly. Beat eggs (as many as you like) and add to skillet and stir as scrambled eggs.

This is some quail that were much more smarter, 'cause they realized they were dead. An' just because they were so smart we fixed this wonderful quail with peach brandy sauce for them.

AIN'T NO QUICHE

8 eggs, beaten
3 cups dry white wine
4 cups cheese, grated
1 tsp. soy sauce
1 TBS. Louisiana hot sauce

2 pie shells, cooked
Onions, bacon, mushrooms,
  pepperoni, or vegetables
Different herbs and spices for flavor

Cool pie shells. Put a layer of grated cheese on bottom of shells; put your onions and mushrooms or bacon and onions on top; put in the dry herbs. Put on more cheese to fill; pour wine and eggs mixture with liquid seasonings on top of cheese mixture to fill—not too full, though. This makes two pie shells full. Bake at 350 degrees for 35 to 45 minutes or until firm and golden brown.

Any gourmet or gourmand know that a quiche will have milk or cream in that. This never saw a cow, so it ain't no quiche.

EGGS JAMBALAYA

Garlic, to taste
Onions, to taste
1/2 to 1 cup mushrooms, chopped

Rice (cooked)
Eggs
1 TBS. soy sauce

Use your leftover rice with amount of eggs you want. Sauté onions and mushrooms in a large frying pan. Add garlic. Beat eggs with soy sauce and pour over onions. Add rice and cook, stirring until the eggs are done as you like them.

You can put as little or as much rice as you like in dis dish. It are good, I garontee!

THANKSGIVING LEFTOVER TURKEY
SAUCE PIQUANT

Baked turkey and/or smoked turkey, deboned
2 cups flour for thick roux
1 cup oil and bacon drippings for roux
2 cups onions, chopped (1 cup white and 1 cup green onions)
1/2 cup celery, chopped (depending on how much turkey)
1/2 cup bell pepper, chopped (same as celery)
1 cup parsley, chopped
2 TBS. garlic, chopped

Salt, to taste
2 TBS. Louisiana hot sauce
2 TBS. Lea & Perrins Worcestershire sauce
Dry white wine (at least 3 cups)
2 to 4 small cans tomato sauce (depends on taste)
Water
Mushrooms (optional), whole
Pimento olives (optional)
6 drops Peychaud's bitters
1/2 tsp. dried mint, crushed

First you make a roux (see my recipe). When the roux is dark brown, add chopped onions, peppers, and celery and continue cooking. When onions become clear, add green onions and parsley and continue cooking for a few minutes. Add a bit of cold water so that the roux becomes a thick liquid. Add chopped garlic and the rest of the seasonings, including tomato sauce and wine. Add turkey and cover with water about 1-1/2 or 2 inches. Bring to a boil, stirring frequently and being sure to have enough water so that sauce piquant won't stick. Cook for several hours, until meat is tender. Serve over spaghetti or rice or just about anything, or by itself.

This is a big recipe. It should feed the whole city (it would feed French Settlement). The reason it's so big is that I want to get that turkey out of my house when Thanksgiving is over.

Game

Deep Fried Venison
Alligator Sauce Piquant
Rabbit Sauce Piquant
Quail in Peach Brandy Sauce
Venison Etouffée
Duck and Turnips
Rabbit and Turnip Etouffée

You can tell I'm not poisoning anybody. I eat what I cook, I garontee.

DEEP FRIED VENISON

Venison (as much as you have)
Salt
Red cayenne pepper

Powdered Worcestershire seasoning
Plain flour
Garlic powder

Clean venison well, being sure to remove fat and membrane. Cut meat into bite-sized pieces about 1 inch by 2 inches. If you cut across the grain, the meat will be more tender.

For two pounds of meat, use about 2 cups of plain flour. Then put as much seasoning in the flour as you like and mix it up.

Roll the chunks of meat in the spicy flour mixture to coat well.

Deep fry the venison chunks until they float and become light brown.

ALLIGATOR SAUCE PIQUANT

5 lbs. alligator meat, chopped in 1-inch cubes
4 cups onions, chopped
1 cup green onions, chopped
1 cup bell pepper, chopped
1 cup parsley, chopped
1/2 cup celery, chopped
2 TBS. garlic, chopped
1 small lemon, chopped fine
6 drops Peychaud's bitters

2 cups plain flour
4 8-oz. cans tomato sauce
1 tsp. dried mint, crushed
4 cups dry white wine
3 TBS. Lea & Perrins Worcestershire
1 TBS. Louisiana hot sauce, or to taste
Cold water, enough to cover
1 cup green pitted olives (optional)
1 lb. mushrooms, fresh (optional)
1 cup oil or bacon drippings

First you make a roux (see my recipe). When the roux is dark brown, add chopped onions, peppers, and celery and continue cooking. When onions become clear, add green onions and parsley and continue cooking a few minutes. Add a bit of cold water so that roux becomes a thick liquid. Add garlic and rest of seasonings, including tomato sauce and wine. Add alligator meat and cover with water about 2 inches over the rest of the ingredients. Bring to a boil, stirring frequently, being sure that you have enough water so that sauce piquant won't stick. Cook for several hours—until meat is tender. Serve over spaghetti or rice or just about anything, or by itself.

RABBIT SAUCE PIQUANT

5 lbs. rabbit, cut in 2-inch cubes
8 medium onions, chopped
2 bunches green onions, chopped
1 large bell pepper, chopped
1 cup celery, chopped
2 8-oz. cans tomato sauce
2 cloves garlic, chopped
2 TBS. Lea & Perrins Worcestershire
   sauce

Juice of 2 lemons
3/4 cup bacon drippings
1 cup all-purpose flour (for roux)
1/2 cup olive oil (for roux)
Salt
6 cups water
Red cayenne pepper
1/4 tsp. Peychaud's bitters
2 cups dry white wine

Wash the rabbit, season with salt and pepper, and fry in bacon drippings until brown. Remove from fat and set aside. Make a roux, using the olive oil and the flour (see my recipe).

Add onions, green onions, bell peppers, and celery to the roux and cook until clear. Add water, wine, garlic, lemon juice, and tomato sauce and stir. Add the rabbit and simmer for 30 minutes, covered. Add bitters and Lea & Perrins and taste for salt and pepper.

Let cook slowly for 2 or more hours.

Serve over rice or spaghetti.

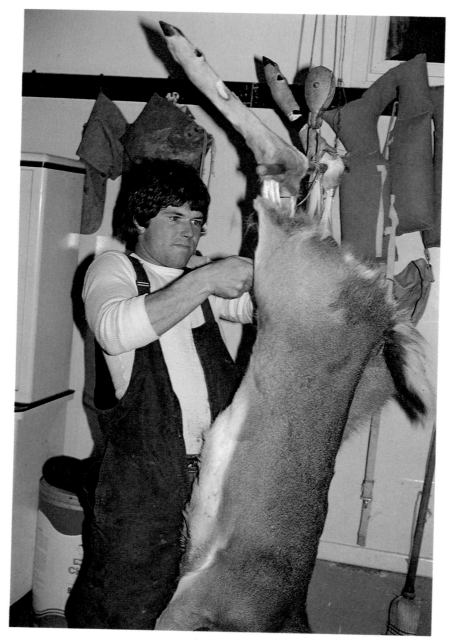

My wife Jeannine's brother, Lane Meeds, dressing out a deer for Jeannine to bring home to me. This was in Montana, the northern part of the Louisiana Purchase.

QUAIL IN PEACH BRANDY SAUCE

2-1/2 lb. quail
1/3 cup peach brandy
1/3 cup claret wine
1 tsp. Seasonall
2 TBS. olive oil

Red pepper
Salt
1 large can peach halves with juice
1 cup parsley, chopped fine

Cut quail down back. Brown in oil, add parsley with salt and pepper and Seasonall. Turn quail, combine brandy, wine, and juice and pour over birds. Cover and simmer 30 minutes.

Serve with peach halves over rice.

VENISON ETOUFFÉE

5 lbs. venison, cut in 1/2-inch cubes
Onions, chopped (by volume, as much as meat)
1 cup bell pepper, chopped
1/2 lemon, chopped fine
2 tsp. garlic, chopped fine
Louisiana hot sauce, to taste

Salt, to taste
2 TBS. Lea & Perrins Worcestershire sauce
1 cup parsley, chopped (1/2 cup if dried)
Olive oil

Salt and pepper meat and brown in olive oil. Put in heavy pot with all the other ingredients. Cook on low heat from 6 to 8 hours until venison is tender. Serve over rice.

Do not add any other liquids, but stir occasionally. By volume, we mean if you have a cup of meat, then you need a cup of onions.

DUCK AND TURNIPS

4 or 3 ducks, cut in 2-inch cubes
1 cup celery, chopped
1 TBS. garlic, chopped
3 cups onions, chopped
1 cup bell pepper, chopped
1 cup green onions, chopped
1 cup parsley, chopped
4 to 6 cups water
3 cups dry white wine
1 TBS. Lea & Perrins Worcestershire
  sauce

1 TBS. soy sauce
1/2 tsp. Peychaud's bitters
1 tsp. dried mint, crushed
Salt
1 TBS. Louisiana hot sauce
8 cups turnips, chopped
1 lemon, chopped fine
1 cup plain flour
1/2 cup olive oil or cooking oil

Brown off ducks and put in a pot big enough to cook the whole dish. Make a roux with the flour and oil (see my recipe). After the roux is made, stir in the chopped onions, celery, and bell pepper and cook until the vegetables are clear. Add the water, wine, and other seasonings. Pour this over the ducks and turnips. Cook 4 to 6 hours over a low fire.

Dis will not feed as many peoples as you might t'ought, 'cause it are dammed good, I garontee.

RABBIT AND TURNIP ETOUFFÉE

Equal amounts by volume of rabbit,
  turnips, and onions
1 cup celery, chopped
1 cup dry white wine
1 to 2 TBS. Lea & Perrins
  Worcestershire sauce

Louisiana hot sauce, to taste
Salt, to taste
1/2 cup dried parsley
2 tsp. garlic, chopped

Put all ingredients together and cook on low heat covered for several hours. Serve over rice.

In a Bag

Baked Onions à la Jeannine
Boned Rump Roast in a Bag
Venison and Turnips in a Bag
St. Patrick's Day Leg of Lamb
Leg of Lamb in a Bag
Fresh Beef Brisket in a Bag
Beef or Pork Ribs Baked in a Bag
Backbone and Turnips in a Bag
Capon in a Cooking Bag
Turkey au Justin in a Bag
Catfish Baked in a Bag

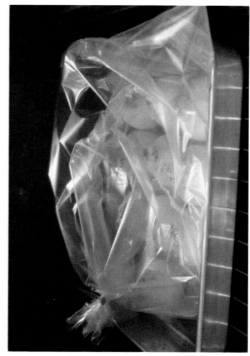

BAKED ONIONS À LA JEANNINE

Dried mint
Medium onions, 1 for each person
Butter

Salt
1 Reynolds cooking bag, turkey-size
1 TBS. flour

Clean onions and cut off ends so onions will stand theyself up straight. Put butter or margarine on top of onions. Put mint or rosemary or any seasoning that you like on top of the margarine. Place in cooking bag that has been shaken with flour. Salt to taste. Seal bag and punch 12 holes in top of bag with a carving fork. Bake at 325 degrees for 1 hour or until onions are tender.

BONED RUMP ROAST IN A BAG

1 TBS. flour
10-lb. beef roast, tied
4 lbs. mushrooms
5 cloves garlic
5 green onions, whole
5 hot pickled peppers
1 cup green onions, chopped
1/2 cup parsley, chopped
2 TBS. soy sauce

8 medium Irish potatoes
1/2 tsp. Peychaud's bitters
Ground red cayenne pepper
Salt
8 large carrots
1 tsp. celery seed
2 cups dry white wine
1 cup water
1 Reynolds cooking bag, turkey-size

Stuff garlic, onions, and peppers in five holes deep in the roast. Clean the mushrooms well. Pat salt and pepper on the roast. Place the roast in a cooking bag with a tablespoon flour shaken up in it. Put the mushrooms, carrots, and potatoes around the roast. Add parsley, green onions, and celery seed. Mix liquids, then pour into the bag.

Tie the bag and punch 12 holes in it with a two-tine kitchen fork. Cook for 1-1/2 hours at 350 degrees.

VENISON AND TURNIPS IN A BAG

Venison roast—whatever you like
Turnips cut into one-inch cubes—as
  many as you like
6 to 10 small onions, whole
1/2 tsp. dried mint
2 TBS. dried parsley
2 cups dry white wine
1 TBS. Lea & Perrins Worcestershire
  sauce

4 drops Peychaud's bitters
Red cayenne pepper, to taste
Salt, to taste
1/2 lb. smoked pork sausage
1/2 tsp. garlic powder
1 TBS. flour
1 Reynolds turkey-cooking bag

Shake flour in bag. Pat salt and pepper on roast. Place roast in bag. Put turnips, onions, and sausage (leave whole—don't cut up) around the roast. Sprinkle the mint and parsley on roast. Dissolve garlic powder in wine and add Lea & Perrins and bitters to wine. Pour into bag (not over the roast). Punch 12 holes in bag with two-tine fork after tying. Cook in 325-degree oven for 2 hours.

SAINT PATRICK'S DAY LEG OF LAMB

1 leg of lamb
1/2 cup crème de menthe
Salt
Cayenne pepper
1 cup onions, chopped
1 TBS. garlic, chopped

2 TBS. Lea & Perrins Worcestershire
  sauce
6 drops Peychaud's bitters
1 cup water
1 TBS. flour
1 turkey-size Reynolds cooking bag

Shake bag with flour in it. Rub salt and pepper into lamb. Then rub crème de menthe into lamb. Put lamb in bag. Pour the leftover crème de menthe over it. Put onions and garlic around it in the bag. Mix water, Lea & Perrins, and bitters. Then pour in the bag (NOT ON THE LAMB). Tie bag and punch 12 holes in it with a carving fork. Cook lamb 1 to 2 hours, depending on how big the leg is and how you like your lamb.

LEG OF LAMB IN A BAG

1 leg of lamb
2 TBS. dried mint
2 cups artichoke hearts
1 lb. whole fresh mushrooms
2 cups onions, chopped
1 TBS. garlic, chopped
1 Reynolds cooking bag, turkey-size

2 cups dry white wine
1 TBS. flour
Red cayenne pepper
Salt
2 TBS. soy sauce
6 drops Peychaud's bitters

Trim most of fat off lamb. Put flour in bag and shake it up really well. Salt and pepper lamb and put mint on it really well. Place lamb in bag. Put onions, garlic, mushrooms, and artichoke hearts around it. Mix rest of ingredients with wine and pour around the lamb—not on it.

Tie bag. Punch 12 holes with fork. Bake in pre-heated oven at 350 degrees for 1 to 2 hours.

FRESH BEEF BRISKET IN A BAG

Beef brisket
Turkey-size Reynolds cooking bag
Cayenne pepper
Salt
Dried mint (crushed)
2 tsp. onion powder

1 tsp. garlic powder
2 TBS. Lea & Perrins Worcestershire
  sauce
1 TBS. plain flour
5 drops Peychaud's bitters
2 cups dry white wine

Salt and pepper brisket. Put flour in bag and shake really well. Put brisket in bag and sprinkle crushed mint on it. Mix wine and all other ingredients, and pour in bag—not on meat. Bake in a preheated oven at 350 degrees for 1 hour.

BEEF OR PORK RIBS BAKED IN A BAG

Reynolds cooking bag, turkey-size
Red cayenne pepper
Dried mint (crushed)
6 to 8 lbs. ribs

2 cups dry white wine
2 cups barbecue sauce
1 TBS. plain flour
Salt

Put flour in bag and shake to coat it. Pat salt and red pepper on ribs, but don't forget to wash your hands after. Put ribs in bag. Combine all other ingredients and mix, then pour into bottom of bag. Seal bag and punch 12 holes with a carving fork. Bake at 325 degrees for about 45 minutes, longer if needed.

This is where I started learning to cook—in the old family home in Amite City, Louisiana.

BACKBONE AND TURNIPS IN A BAG

6 to 8 cups turnips, chopped
3 lbs. pork backbone, cut up in 2-inch
    cubes
2 TBS. flour
2 cups onions, chopped
1 cup bell pepper, chopped
1/2 cup celery, chopped
1 tsp. garlic, minced
1/2 cup parsley, chopped
1 TBS. Lea & Perrins Worcestershire
    sauce

Cayenne pepper
1 TBS. soy sauce
1 TBS. Kitchen Bouquet
Salt
3 cups dry white wine
1 cup water
1/4 tsp. Peychaud's bitters
1 Reynolds turkey-size cooking bag

Shake up flour in bag. Salt and pepper backbone and put into bag. Put turnips, onions, bell pepper, celery, and garlic in bag. Mix Lea & Perrins, soy sauce, Kitchen Bouquet, wine, bitters, and water and pour in bag. Salt to taste. Seal bag and punch 12 holes with carving fork. Bake at 350 degrees for 2 hours.

CAPON IN A COOKING BAG

Reynolds turkey-size cooking bag
1 TBS. plain flour
1 capon or big chicken
6 peeled Irish potatoes, medium-size
6 whole onions
6 whole carrots
3 whole bell peppers, quartered
2 cloves garlic (one for inside and one
    for outside capon)

2 cups dry white wine
1 cup water
1-1/2 tsp. dried mint, crushed
1 TBS. dried parsley
2 TBS. Lea & Perrins Worcestershire
    sauce
Red cayenne pepper
Salt

Shake flour in bag to coat it. Pat capon with salt and red cayenne pepper. Put into bag and put vegetables around bird. Mix the seasonings with the wine and pour into the bottom of the bag. Seal bag and punch 12 holes with carving fork. Bake about 1-1/2 hours at 350 degrees.

TURKEY AU JUSTIN IN A BAG

1 TBS. flour
Turkey
Olive oil
Onions, chopped
Parsley, chopped
2 cloves garlic (one for inside and one
    for outside bird)

1 cup dry white wine
Water
Cayenne pepper
Salt
Reynolds turkey-size cooking bag

Shake up flour in bag. Rub olive oil on turkey really well. Pepper and salt turkey, then place in bag. Put chopped onions, parsley, and garlic around turkey and add wine and water. Seal bag and punch 12 holes with carving fork. Bake at 325 degrees until brown.

CATFISH BAKED IN A BAG

6 to 10 lbs. of thick catfish fillet
Cooking bag, turkey-size
1 TBS. flour

Lemon Butter Sauce:
1 lb. oleo
1 tsp. onion powder
1 TBS. Lea & Perrins Worcestershire
    sauce

2 tsp. Louisiana hot sauce
Juice of two lemons
Juice of two limes
1 cup dry white wine
2 tsp. salt
Cayenne pepper

Sprinkle fish with cayenne pepper and salt. Put flour in cooking bag and shake. Put fish in bag and pour lemon butter sauce around it. Seal bag and punch 12 holes in top of bag with a carving fork. Bake 30 minutes at 350 degrees.

Vegetables

Navy Beans with Smoked Sausage
La Sauce Patat (Stewed Potatoes)
Stewed Okra
Okra and Tomatoes
Fried Eggplant
Asparagus and Pecans
Baked Beans
Collards au Vin
Barbecued Beans
Turnips au Gratin
Turnips Bourguignon
Oven-Baked Leftover Peas
Leftover Rice and Peas
Artichoke Heart Casserole
Leftover Stewed Okra
Ripe Tomato Casserole au Justin
Sweet Potato Casserole
Mirliton or Choyote or Vegetable Pear Casserole with Crabmeat
Okra Succotash
Fresh Snap Beans, or Green Beans au Vin
Cabbage au Vin au Mushrooms

When I get through with these Justin Wilson mustard greens, cooking them in wine, people who never ate them before will steal them out of you plate.

NAVY BEANS WITH SMOKED SAUSAGE

1 lb. navy beans
1 cup onions, chopped
1 TBS. garlic, chopped
1 cayenne pepper or 1 tsp. Louisiana
   hot sauce

2 cups dry white wine
Water to cover about 2 inches
Olive oil to brown meat
1/4 lb. pickled shoulder or salt meat
2 lbs. smoked sausage

Soak beans overnight in wine, water, and seasonings. Brown meat. Put beans and water with seasonings in pot, then put smoked sausage and cook until beans are tender.

Man, dis are too good to put a describe on it!

LA SAUCE PATAT
(Stewed Potatoes au Murphy Brown)

Plenty bacon, chopped
Plenty onions, chopped
Little bell pepper, chopped
Little celery, chopped
Irish potatoes, sliced, as many as the
   pot will hold

Salt
Red pepper (and black, if you want it)
Plenty green onions, chopped
Plenty parsley, chopped

The amounts of ingredients will depend on the size of the pot used. Fry the bacon. Add onions, bell pepper, and celery. Add thinly sliced potatoes. Salt and pepper to taste. Put green onions and parsley in last. Cook over medium heat until potatoes are soft (even mushy). Stir frequently.

Dis is actual stewed patat.

La Sauce Patat festival holds forth at French Settlement, Louisiana, in July every year.

STEWED OKRA

———————◆———————

4 or 3 cups okra, chopped
1 cup onions, chopped
1/2 cup parsley, chopped fine
1/2 cup bell pepper, chopped
1 tsp. garlic, chopped

1/2 lb. bacon, diced
Salt, to taste
1 TBS. soy sauce
1 TBS. Louisiana hot sauce

Fry bacon. Add all ingredients. Simmer until onions are tender. Stir often.

OKRA AND TOMATOES

———————◆———————

4 cups okra, chopped
2 cans tomatoes
1 cup onion, chopped
1 can Ro-tel
3 TBS. soy sauce

4 tsp. Louisiana hot sauce
1 clove garlic, chopped
1/2 lb. bacon, diced
2 TBS. parsley flakes
6 drops Peychaud's bitters

Fry the okra to get slime out. If you don't know what I mean by this, get some fresh okra, slice it, and put it in a frying pan—it got slime and it need to be deslimified. Add tomatoes, Ro-tel, and fried bacon and seasonings to bacon drippings and deslimed okra. Cook slowly until onions are done, stirring frequently.

FRIED EGGPLANT

3 small eggplants
3 TBS. olive oil or more
Flour
Salt, red cayenne pepper, garlic
   powder, and onion powder

4 medium eggs, beaten
1 cup dry white wine
Romano cheese to sprinkle when done

Beat together wine and eggs. Slice eggplant 1/4- to 1/2-inch thick. Soak in water and dry. Dredge eggplant slices in egg and wine. Then dredge in spiced flour mixture. Fry in olive oil and sprinkle with Romano cheese. Serve immediately.

ASPARAGUS AND PECANS

2 lbs. fresh asparagus
Water
1 cup dry white wine
Salt to taste
1/2 cup olive oil

Cayenne pepper
1/4 cup fresh lemon juice
1 TBS. soy sauce
3/4 cup pecans, chopped

Boil asparagus in water, wine, and salt until tender. Then drain and place in a covered casserole. Sprinkle with cayenne pepper. Pour olive oil over this, then lemon juice. Add pecans and soy sauce. Mix as much as possible and place in 300-degree oven for 45 minutes.

Snap beans au vin with ham hocks looks good . . . o-o-o-h boy . . . but tastes much more better than it looks.

This is turnips au gratin. Pore little turnips—some people just don't know how good they are.

BAKED BEANS

———————◆———————

2 lbs. white beans (navy beans)
2 cups dry white wine
1/4 lb. bacon, chopped
Louisiana hot sauce, to taste
2 TBS. steak sauce
1 TBS. dried parsley
6 drops Peychaud's bitters
Strips of bacon to garnish top

1 cup honey
16-oz. bottle catsup
1 TBS. wine vinegar
1/2 cup yellow mustard
1 tsp. dried mint, crushed
1 TBS. mustard seed
Water

Fry off bacon chips. After washing beans, cook in mixture of wine, water, Louisiana hot sauce, mint, parsley, bitters, and salt. Cook until tender, then place in roaster. Mix honey, catsup (rinse bottle with vinegar), mustard, steak sauce, and mustard seed and blend into beans in roaster. Strip with bacon on top. Cook at 350 degrees for 4 to 6 hours. Keep open until not too juicy, then place cover on roaster.

COLLARDS AU VIN

———————◆———————

2 cups dry white wine (at least)
Lots of cut up collards (they cook
    down)
1 cup onions, chopped
Pickled shoulder or salt meat

Water, enough to cover collards about
    1 to 2 inches
Salt, Louisiana hot sauce or a fresh
    hot pepper

Brown meat in pot. Add other ingredients and bring to a boil. Then reduce fire and simmer for about 1 hour. Stir occasionally.

BARBECUED BEANS

2 lbs. beans
2 cups dry white wine
1 clove garlic, chopped
1 cup onions, chopped
1/2 tsp. dried mint, crushed
6 drops Peychaud's bitters
Pickled pork or salt pork—large cubes

Water
2 TBS. bacon drippings
Salt
1/2 cup bell peppers, chopped
1 hot pepper, chopped
2 tsp. liquid smoke

Marinate beans overnight with all seasonings. Cover with wine and water. (Beans may swell, so when they are cooked, water may have to be added.) Brown pickled pork or salt pork in bacon drippings. Add the beans with marinating liquid. Cook until tender, then salt to taste.

TURNIPS AU GRATIN

6 to 8 large turnips, sliced
Olive oil
6 to 8 large onions, sliced
2 cups dry white wine
4 eggs, beaten
Salt

2 tsp. red cayenne pepper, or
    Louisiana hot sauce
3 cups Swiss, cheddar, Parmesan
    and/or Romano cheese, grated
Sliced cheese for top

Grease casserole with oil. Layer onions, turnips, and cheeses in casserole. Beat eggs, adding wine and putting in spices. Pour liquids over casserole and place cheese on top. Bake 1 to 1-1/2 hours at 350 degrees, or until turnips are tender.

TURNIPS BOURGUIGNON

Awful yech!

4 cups turnips, peeled and cubed
1 cup dry red wine
1/2 cup onions, chopped
1/2 cup bacon drippings or salt pork
    meat

1 tsp. sugar
1 tsp. salt
1 tsp. Louisiana hot sauce

Put all ingredients in a pot and cook over low heat until turnips are tender.

OVEN-BAKED LEFTOVER PEAS

English peas, or green peas, or
    black-eyed peas, or field peas, or
    crowder peas, cooked with onions
    and garlic
Honey
Garlic powder
Onion powder
Louisiana hot sauce
Catsup
Mustard seed
Bacon, stripped

Combine all of these ingredients except bacon with leftover peas. Strip the bacon on top. Bake in a 325-degree oven until bacon is browned.

Too many peoples don't use leftover peas, and dat's bad—try dis, you'll lak it.

LEFTOVER RICE AND PEAS
(Blackeyed or Any Kind)

Rice, whatever is left over
Peas, whatever is left over
1/2 lb. soft-fried bacon bits or cubes
1/2 tsp. mustard seed
1 tsp. onion powder
1/2 tsp. garlic powder
Grated cheddar cheese, enough to
    cover top
Parmesan or Romano cheese, grated
    (small amount)
1/4 cup dried parsley
1 TBS. soy sauce
Louisiana hot sauce, to taste
Eggs, beaten with dry white wine (2, 4,
    or 6—depending on how much left-
    overs you have)

Combine all these ingredients and top with cheddar cheese. Bake at 325 degrees for 45 minutes to 1 hour.

One of my tester-tasters beat the photographer to the draw on this picture of an artichoke heart casserole.

ARTICHOKE HEART CASSEROLE

1/2 cup dry white wine
4 cans artichoke hearts
1/4 cup olive oil
1 tsp. onion powder
1/2 tsp. garlic powder

Red cayenne pepper, to taste
Salt, to taste
1 cup Parmesan or Romano cheese, grated
2 cups seasoned bread crumbs

Grease casserole with olive oil. Quarter artichoke hearts. Mix with all ingredients. Place in casserole, sprinkle bread crumbs on top, and bake in 350-degree oven for 30 minutes.

LEFTOVER STEWED OKRA

Leftover okra
Eggs (equal to amount of okra)

Assorted cheeses, grated

Put okra in dish, beat eggs, and pour over top. Put cheese over top and bake until cheese is melted and okra is heated through.

Don't t'row dat leftover okra away. Try dis.

RIPE TOMATO CASSEROLE AU JUSTIN

Olive oil
6 ripe tomatoes, sliced thick
3 onions, sliced thin
2 tsp. salt

1 tsp. Seasonall
1 cup Romano cheese, grated
6 slices bacon
1 cup seasoned bread crumbs

Grease casserole with olive oil. Layer casserole with ripe tomatoes, onions, salt, Seasonall, and cheese. Top with bread crumbs and fried bacon. Bake 1 hour at 325 degrees.

SWEET POTATO CASSEROLE
(Yam)

3 lbs. yams (canned or freshly
   cooked), drained
1 cup pecans, chopped and whole
1 #2 can crushed pineapple

1 cup moist grated coconut
1 cup honey
Marshmallows

Mix first 5 ingredients together. Be careful not to get too much juice from yams. Cover top with marshmallows and bake at 325 degrees until marshmallows are brown—approximately 45 minutes.

This is a vegetable dish but it tastes like a dessert.

MIRLITON, OR CHOYOTE, OR VEGETABLE PEAR CASSEROLE WITH CRABMEAT

1 lb. crabmeat
1 cup onions, chopped
1 size #300 can ripe olives and 1/2 can
   juice
8 cups mirlitons, peeled and sliced
3 drops Peychaud's bitters
1 cup dry white wine

Louisiana hot sauce, to taste
1 tsp. dill seed
1/2 tsp. mint (dried)
4 eggs, beaten
1 TBS. soy sauce
1 tsp. salt
Seasoned bread crumbs

Combine all ingredients and cover with bread crumbs. Bake at 350 degrees until mirliton is tender.

This is a vegetable which got some alias. That mean it taste so good, it's criminal and goes by three different names.

OKRA SUCCOTASH

1 cup onions, chopped
1 cup bell pepper, chopped (and hot
    pepper if you have it)
1 TBS. garlic, chopped

1 can (16 oz.) tomatoes, mashed
3 cups okra, chopped
1 can (16 oz.) whole kernel corn
Salt and pepper, to taste

Put all of the ingredients in a big pot and cook until the okra and the onions are done. Serve it over rice.

How many will it serve? I don't know. It depends on how many are coming and how hungry they are!

FRESH SNAP BEANS, OR GREEN BEANS AU VIN

2 lbs. fresh snap beans
1/2 cup olive oil
2 slices thick bacon, cubed
2 medium-sized onions, chopped
1 small clove garlic, chopped
3 or 2 cups dry white wine

1 TBS. Lea & Perrins Worcestershire
    sauce
Louisiana hot sauce (cayenne)
Salt
Water, if needed

Snap and clean the beans. Pour the olive oil into a pot big enough to hold all the beans with ease. Put bacon in olive oil and fry until soft, not brown. Add beans, onions, garlic, and wine. Add Lea & Perrins and season with Louisiana hot sauce to taste. Approximately 1 to 2 teaspoons should do. After beans have become tender, salt to taste and cook until done to your taste. Serves 8.

CABBAGE AU VIN AU MUSHROOMS

2 medium heads cabbage, sliced or
    quartered
1 cup onions, chopped
2 tsp. garlic, chopped
1/2 tsp. dried mint
2 cups dry white wine
1/2 lb. salt shoulder, or smoked pig
    tail, or pickled pork

Louisiana hot sauce or red pepper, to
    taste
1 lb. fresh mushrooms, washed
Water to nearly cover
Salt, if necessary

Brown meat a little. Put cabbage in deep pot along with mushrooms. Pour in wine, water, and all seasonings. Bring to a boil and then simmer slowly until the cabbage is tender.

Smoker Cooker

General Directions
Smoked Ducks
Smoked Beef Roast or Pork Roast
Smoked Turkey
Oysters in Smoker Cooker
Smoked Venison Roast
Fish in Smoker Cooker
Smoked Chicken Twins
Leg of Lamb with Porkloin in Double Smoker Cooker
Alligator Tail in Smoker Cooker

SMOKER COOKER

GENERAL DIRECTIONS

━━━━◆━━━━

I use the Cookin' Cajun Water Smoker because it works the best for me.

First of all, use good, dry charcoal briquets, not damp ones. Use starter and let the fire catch well until the edges of a good bit of the charcoal become white before you put the pieces of wood on it.

To make the flavorful smoke, I suggest pieces of hickory, pecan, or walnut wood that have been soaked in water for at least an hour. The soaking makes the pieces of wood produce more smoke and burn longer.

While your fire is getting started, put the seasoning listed below in the water pan, but don't put the water in at this time or you will spill it on your coals and put your fire out.

I usually sprinkle salt over the entire surface of the food to be cooked and pat it into the surface. Then I do the same with red cayenne pepper. I always wash my hands after this step. If you don't wash your hands, you will find out why I do. Don't scratch yourself anywhere, let alone the wrong place.

BASIC SEASONING FOR THE WATER SMOKER
(to put into the water pan)

1 cup dry white wine	**6 drops Peychaud's bitters**
1 bell pepper, halved and cleaned	**1 medium onion, whole**
2 TBS. dried parsley	**1 clove garlic, whole**
2 TBS. Lea & Perrins Worcestershire sauce	**1 tsp. dried mint, crushed**
	1 TBS. Liquid Smoke

For seafood, I usually use a halved lemon instead of dried mint. Or you can experiment with other wines and seasonings.

Also, I usually put two meats on my Cookin' Cajun at one time. For example, I put a big pork roast on the top rack when I cook a beef roast on the bottom rack. As the meats cook, the fat from the pork roast drips down onto the beef and keeps it moist. The tasty juices from the meats drip into the water pan and make a great "jus" gravy. Or I may cook a turkey on the bottom and a ham on the top. The fatty meat makes the leaner meat more moist.

Be careful not to overcook meats or fish because they will get too dry.

SMOKED DUCKS

Clean ducks well, leaving the skin on them. Prepare smoker cooker with the following seasonings in the water pan:

1 cup dry white wine
1 onion, whole
1 apple, halved
1 turnip, halved
1 TBS. Liquid Smoke

1 tsp. dried mint, crushed
1 TBS. parsley, chopped
6 drops Peychaud's bitters
1 TBS. Lea & Perrins Worcestershire sauce

Put an apple or turnip or onion or all of these inside the ducks. Salt and pepper well inside and out. Put in Cookin' Cajun, being very careful not to overcook.

SMOKED BEEF ROAST OR PORK ROAST

20 lb. beef roast
10–20 cloves garlic, whole

10–20 cayenne peppers, whole
10–20 green onions, whole

Prepare the Cookin' Cajun with the following seasonings in the water pan:

1 cup dry white or dry red wine
1 onion, whole
1 clove garlic, whole
1 TBS. Liquid Smoke
1 tsp. dried mint, crushed

2 TBS. parsley, chopped
6 drops Peychaud's bitters
2 TBS. Lea & Perrins Worcestershire sauce

Stick a knife into the meat, making a deep puncture. With finger, push 1 clove garlic in the hole and then a long pepper and a green onion. Slice off the pepper and the onion even with the surface of the meat. Do this over the entire piece of meat. Sprinkle the meat with salt and red pepper and put on the bottom rack of the smoker cooker under a pork roast. Fill the cooker all the way with briquets and water. I usually put these on about 11 P.M. and let them cook while I sleep.

The gravy that is left in the water pan is delicious.

Alligator tail soaking in ice to drain blood.

Alligator tail sauce piquant.

SMOKED TURKEY

Prepare smoker. While briquets are starting to burn, sprinkle carcass and cavity with salt and red pepper. I put a whole onion inside the cavity, but you can make a stuffing if you like. Be careful not to use ingredients in the stuffing that will spoil too quickly.

Seasonings That Go in the Water Pan

1 cup dry white wine
1 onion, whole
1 clove garlic, whole
1 TBS. Liquid Smoke
1 tsp. dried mint, crushed

2 TBS. parsley, chopped
6 drops Peychaud's bitters
2 TBS. Lea & Perrins Worcestershire
sauce

I put a pork roast on the top rack of my Cookin' Cajun and a turkey on the bottom rack. Then I fill the water pan plumb up and let it cook while I sleep at night.

OYSTERS IN SMOKER COOKER

Oysters, enough to cover screen
Salt oysters in their own juice

Seasonings That Go in the Water Pan

1 cup dry white wine
1 TBS. Liquid Smoke
1 lemon, cut up
1 TBS. dried parsley

Juice of oysters
Charcoal—not too much—2 or 3 lbs.
Hickory or pecan wood—2 or 3 small
pieces

Soak wood in water. Light charcoal. Let it burn down, then place wood on charcoal. Put water pan with wine, Liquid Smoke, parsley, and lemon in smoker cooker. Add juice from oysters. Fill about half full with water. Place oysters on greased screen on grill and put in smoker cooker. Close cooker and cook for about 1 to 2 hours, but check it every now and then.

SMOKED VENISON ROAST

————◆•◆————

Prepare the Cookin' Cajun as you would for any other roast. Put the ingredients listed below in the water pan:

1 cup dry white wine	**1 tsp. dried mint, crushed**
1 medium onion, whole	**6 drops Peychaud's bitters**
1 bell pepper, halved and peeled	**2 TBS. Lea & Perrins Worcestershire**
1 large clove garlic, whole	**sauce**
2 TBS. dried parsley	**1 TBS. liquid smoke**

To cook venison, it is important to remove the fat and membrane from the meat.

I stick a knife in the meat, then push some peeled cloves of garlic into the slit. You can push whole fresh cayenne peppers and green onions in the slit also.

After stuffing the slits you have made, sprinkle salt over the surface and pat it in. Do the same with red cayenne pepper.

I would smoke the venison on the bottom rack and put a pork roast on the top rack of the Cookin' Cajun. That way it won't be so dry.

FISH IN SMOKER COOKER

————◆•◆————

1 layer of fish on screen (fillets or whole fish)

Seasonings That Go in the Water Pan

1 cup dry white wine	**Red cayenne pepper**
1 TBS. Liquid Smoke	**Water**
1 lemon, cut up	**Charcoal—not too much—about 3 lbs.**
1 TBS. dried parsley	**Hickory or pecan wood—2 or 3 pieces**
Salt	

Salt and pepper fish. Soak wood in water. Light charcoal and let burn down, then place wood on charcoal. Put water pan with wine, liquid smoke, parsley, and lemon in smoker cooker. Fill pan with water, being careful not to splash on fire. Place fish on greased screen over grill. Close smoker cooker and smoke for about 2 hours. Check to see if done before the 2 hours are up.

SMOKED CHICKEN TWINS
(Not Identical, No)

———————◆———————

2 baking hens

STUFFING

1 cup green onions, chopped
1/2 cup bell pepper, chopped
1/2 cup parsley, chopped
1/2 cup celery, chopped
Dried bread or old toast
4 eggs, beaten
2 tsp. Louisiana hot sauce
1 TBS. Lea & Perrins Worcestershire
   sauce

8 drops Peychaud's bitters
2 cups or more of dry white wine
1 cup water
1/2 tsp. dried mint, crushed
Smoked sausage, sliced
Italian sausage, sliced
Smoked or fresh oysters (optional)

Mix dressing with vegetables, bread, eggs, seasonings, and wine. Make 1/2 with smoked sausage and 1/2 with Italian sausage. Stuff the twins full.

Prepare smoker with these seasonings in the water pan:

1 cup dry white wine
1 onion, whole
1 clove garlic, whole
1 TBS. Liquid Smoke
1 tsp. dried mint, crushed

2 TBS. parsley, chopped
6 drops Peychaud's bitters
2 TBS. Lea & Perrins Worcestershire
   sauce

Light charcoal and let it burn down. Put soaked wood chips on briquets. Put in water pan and fill with water. Put chicken twins on rack and smoke about 5 hours.

Sit yourself down and eat. This is ready.

LEG OF LAMB WITH PORKLOIN
IN DOUBLE SMOKER COOKER

1 leg of lamb
1 small porkloin
Fresh mint
Salt
Cayenne pepper
1 cup dry white wine
1 tsp. dried mint, crushed

1 large clove garlic, whole
1 TBS. Lea & Perrins Worcestershire
   sauce
1 large onion, peeled and whole
Water
5 to 7 lbs. charcoal
3 or 4 pieces pecan or hickory wood

Salt and pepper pork and lamb (remove most of fat from lamb). Pat fresh mint on lamb, trying to make it stick as much as possible. Put wine, dried mint, garlic, Lea & Perrins, and onion in water pan. Light charcoal, let it burn down, then place wood on it. Put water pan in smoker cooker and add water carefully until pan is filled. Place lamb on bottom grill, pork on top grill. Close cooker and cook for approximately 4 to 5 hours. Check to see if pork is coming away from bone. If it is, the meat is done.

ALLIGATOR TAIL IN SMOKER COOKER

When I get my alligator tail, I put it in a cooler with ice and let it soak to leach out the blood. I pour off the ice water and put more ice on it. After about 2 days, the meat is nice and white.

Then get the smoker cooker ready following my general directions with these seasonings in the water pan.

1 cup dry white wine
1 medium onion, whole
1 lemon, halved
1 bell pepper, whole
2 TBS. Lea & Perrins Worcestershire
   sauce

2 TBS. dried parsley
6 drops Peychaud's bitters
1 TBS. liquid smoke

Sprinkle and pat the outside of the meat with salt and cayenne pepper. Cook 8 to 10 hours, depending on the size of the tail.

Desserts

Raisin Supreme au Justin
Fruit Cup à la Jeannine
Cookies
Fruit Pies
Applesauce
Pound Cake
Rice Pudding Falernum
Strawberry Cheesecake
Rita's Texas Chocolate Pie

This is fruit cup à la Jeannine, and it is much more better than good; it is delicious.

RAISIN SUPREME AU JUSTIN

6 to 8 cups seedless raisins
1 cup brandy
1 cup Benedictine

1/2 cup honey
1 tsp. cinnamon
1/4 tsp. Peychaud's bitters

Put all the ingredients in a pan on the stove and bring to a boil (not a rolling boil). Simmer, covered, for 2 hours.

This delicious supreme can be put over ice cream, lemon pie, or even vanilla wafers for a tasty treat.

FRUIT CUP À LA JEANNINE

A variety of fresh fruits in bite-sized pieces:

Mandarin oranges
Pineapple chunks
Seedless grapes
Strawberries
Apples
Bananas
Cherries (pitted)

Melons
Honey
Plain yogurt
Cinnamon
Chopped nuts (optional)
Grated coconut (optional)

Put all fruit in a bowl and mix lightly. Make a sauce out of the yogurt, a bit of honey, and a bit of ground cinnamon. Dish fruit into champagne glasses or bowls and drizzle yogurt mixture on top.

COOKIES

2 cups oatmeal

1 cup sugar

1 cup butter or margarine

5 or 6 TBS. cocoa

Enough water to moisten

Mix ingredients together with hands and shape into balls. Roll in confectioner's sugar.

FRUIT PIES

Cut up apples, or peaches, or plums, or pears, or figs, or nectarines, thin

2 9-inch pie shells

1/4 cup sugar for each pie

Ground cinnamon, to taste

Lemon juice or 1 lemon for each pie

Put fruit in bottom pie crust and squeeze lemon over fruit. Sprinkle with sugar and cinnamon and put on top pie crust. Bake at 400 degrees for few minutes to set crust, and then at 325 degrees until brown.

Notice we say, "or"—don't try to use all the fruits in one pie.

APPLESAUCE

Take all the apples in the house that are about to go bad.

6 to 8 cups apples, peeled, cored, and quartered
Cover bottom of pot with 3/4 inch water

Put apples in pot
1/2 cup sugar
Sprinkle with cinnamon
2 TBS. lemon juice

Bring to a boil. Then simmer until it is practically apple butter.

POUND CAKE

1 cup butter or margarine
3 cups sugar
1/2 tsp. salt
1/2 cup salad oil
5 large eggs

3/4 tsp. vanilla extract
3/4 tsp. butter extract
1 cup sweet milk
3 2/3 cups flour

Cream butter, add sugar, and cream well together. Add salad oil (about 2 teaspoons at a time). Add eggs, one at a time, beating after each addition. Add flavoring and salt. Add milk and flour alternately. Beat well. Bake in a greased tube pan at 325 degrees for 1 hour and 25 minutes. Remove from pan and cool on cake rack.

You can use any flavoring you like, but we like this as a butter *pound cake.*

Fred Porche, a real sausage maker, is not listening to one word of advice I'm giving him.

RICE PUDDING FALERNUM

3 cups cooked rice
4 TBS. cream cheese
2 TBS. honey
1/3 cup falernum

1/4 cup warm water to rinse out
 falernum
1/2 cup seedless raisins
1/2 cup pecans, chopped

Blend honey, falernum, and cream cheese and water. Add to rice and raisins and pecans, mix thoroughly. Place in 325-degree oven in open casserole dish for 1 hour.

Falernum is a flavoring made by the Sazerac Company in New Orleans, Louisiana. It has an unusual flavor, and all I have to do is smell it to start conjurateing recipes that use falernum. I use it on chicken, and the best homemade ice cream I ever had was falernum ice cream.

STRAWBERRY CHEESECAKE

Crust

1 cup self-rising flour
1 cup crushed pecans

1/2 cup brown sugar
1 cup melted butter

Combine all ingredients and press into the bottom of a 9-inch square baking pan. Bake in 400-degree oven for 10 to 15 minutes. Let cool.

Filling

1 lb. Cool Whip
2 lbs. cream cheese
2 TBS. sugar

1 TBS. falernum
1 lb. sweet, ripe strawberries

Combine softened cream cheese with Cool Whip and beat until smooth, adding sugar and falernum gradually. Add half of the strawberries to the cheese mixture and beat until it is pink. Put filling into crust. Place remainder of strawberries on top.

I like to experiment with this recipe. You can use any kind of fruit, not just strawberries. You can leave the fruit and falernum out, which would give you a plain cheesecake. Then top it with fruit.

You can also use other kinds of nuts for the crust—walnuts or almonds, for example. For a different kind of cheesecake, try crushed peanuts for the crust and add chocolate to the cream cheese. You'll get Peanut Butter Cup Cheesecake.

RITA'S TEXAS CHOCOLATE PIE

Crust

1-1/2 cups plain flour
1-1/2 sticks butter, melted

2 TBS. powdered sugar (heaping spoons)
3/4 cup pecans, chopped fine

Mix and pat into 9-by-13 pan. Bake at 350 degrees for 20 minutes.

Filling

1-1/2 cups sugar
1/3 cup cornstarch
3 cups milk
4 egg yolks, slightly beaten

1/4 tsp. salt
2 oz. melted unsweetened chocolate
1 tsp. vanilla

Stir the sugar, cornstarch, and salt together in a double boiler. Blend egg yolks and milk, and add to the sugar mixture. Cook until thick. Remove from heat, add vanilla and chocolate, and let cool. Put into crust. Spread top with whipped cream or Cool Whip and sprinkle with toasted coconut.

INDEX